ADVERTISING
for the small business

how to get maximum sales
for the minimum cost

second edition

ADVERTISING
for the small business

how to get maximum sales
for the minimum cost

second edition

N I C K D A W S

Otter Publications
Chichester, England

© Copyright Otter Publications 2000

First published in 1996 by Otter Publications
ISBN 1 899053 08 5

This second edition published in 2000 by Otter Publications, 9 Roman
Way, Fishbourne, Chichester, West Sussex, PO19 3QN.

DISCLAIMER

British Library Cataloging in Publication Data
A CIP record for this book is available from the British Library.
ISBN 1 899053 14 X

Text design by Bookman.
Cover design by Sara Howell.
All cartoons by Simon Golding.
Printed and bound in Great Britain.
Distributed in the UK by Gardners Books, Eastbourne.

*The Otter Publications logo is reproduced from
original artwork by David Kitt.*

CONTENTS

INTRODUCTION

In the UK alone over £9 billion a year is spent on advertising. Some of this money is spent on their clients' behalf by advertising agencies, but by far the greater proportion is spent by businesses themselves. Some of these are large corporations, but many more are small businesses employing no more than a dozen or so staff, and self-employed people. While their individual advertising budgets may be small, in total they exceed those of multi-nationals such as Shell or ICI. These are the people for whom this book has been written. It is also for those who are planning to start a business, but have not yet begun to trade.

ADVERTISING FOR THE SMALL BUSINESS is very much a practical guide. I have deliberately kept theory to a minimum, while concentrating on providing the practical assistance which - in my experience - small businesses most require. I have assumed that most readers will be responsible for arranging their own advertising. The work of agencies is covered, therefore, but not in great detail.

Most people in small businesses have tight budgets, especially when first starting out. So the emphasis throughout this book is on getting value for money - or, as the sub-title expresses it, how to get maximum sales for the minimum cost. Hence you will find in these pages many tips on making your advertising budget go further. There is, for example, a chapter on low-cost classified ads - a subject many books on advertising barely mention, despite the fact that people have become millionaires through this medium alone.

Other chapters cover display advertising, sales letters, direct response, public relations, sales promotions, point-of-sale advertising, and so on - all forms of advertising which small businesses can effectively exploit. In contrast, TV, film and billboard advertising have not been covered in depth, as these are mainly handled by agencies, and are in any case likely to be outside the budgets of most small businesses.

As many of the same principles apply to different forms of advertising, you may notice that certain points are repeated in different chapters. I am sorry if any readers find this irritating. I have done it simply to avoid the inconvenience of constantly referring readers backwards and forwards through the book. And, of course, repetition is a highly effective way of fixing important points in the mind!

ADVERTISING FOR THE SMALL BUSINESS has been written for non-specialists, so I have tried to keep jargon to a minimum. This is not always easy in a creative field such as advertising, which has spawned enough specialist terms to fill a fair-sized dictionary. Where such terms are needed I have tried to explain them in the text. In addition, at the end of the book you will find a detailed glossary.

I am conscious that I am addressing a diverse readership of builders, draughtsmen, shop owners, computer programmers, small manufacturers, caterers, graphic artists, plumbers, taxi drivers, mail order operators, and so on. I have therefore used general terms such as 'the product', 'the service' and 'the business' to cover the entire range, while including plenty of specific examples to illustrate the points made. In fact, this is not so much of a problem as might be imagined. While advertising takes many forms and can have a range of purposes, as I have already mentioned, the underlying principles remain much the same whatever the field.

At the end of each chapter is a list of key points. This serves a number of purposes. It assists the learning process by repeating the most important points which have been made; it provides a brief summary of the information given; and it can be used subsequently as a quick reference guide or index to the chapter. With the longer chapters (e.g. Sales Letters) in particular, you may find it useful to study the list of key points before reading the chapter itself, to gain an overview of the material covered. This is, in any event, good educational practice.

Finally, to counter any accusations of sexism, I admit I have used the first person pronoun he (or him) throughout this book. This is not from any wish to discriminate against women, simply a consequence of the fact that the English language lacks a third-person singular pronoun which covers both sexes. Rather than write 'he/she' or the even uglier 's/he' on every occasion, I have therefore decided to take the simplest path and use 'he' throughout. I hope my female readers will understand this and not be offended by it. Advertising is, of course, a field in which many women excel, and an increasing number of successful entrepreneurs are female.

CHAPTER ONE

PRINCIPLES OF ADVERTISING

Before getting down to examining practical aspects of advertising, we need to spend a little time looking at its role in the overall context of running a business. Advertising, of course, usually aims to attract new customers to a business. But advertising alone cannot guarantee sales. To see why this is so, we need to look at the larger concept of marketing, of which advertising is just a part.

WHAT IS MARKETING?

In many people's minds, marketing is no more than a fancy name for selling. It is associated with goods such as beer, breakfast cereals and toiletries, or more expensive products such as washing machines, video recorders and package holidays. With such a widespread misconception, it is easy to get the impression that marketing is an expensive, large company activity, not really applicable to the small business.

In fact, nothing could be further from the truth. Marketing is vital to every business, no matter how small. Advertising, selling and other promotional activities are important, but they are only a small part of what marketing is about. To understand this, it may help to consider a definition from the Institute of Marketing (IOM)...

"Marketing is the management process responsible for identifying, anticipating and satisfying customer requirements profitably."

It is easy to fall into the trap of seeing your business in terms of the products and services you provide, with advertising as the means by which you will persuade people to buy. However, the IOM definition emphasises that no amount of advertising can persuade people to buy products they neither want nor need.

The Institute of Marketing definition shows that marketing starts from quite a different point of view. It begins not with the products or services, but with customers, who have a range of requirements they want satisfied. Marketing involves identifying what these requirements are, and satisfying them by developing and adapting the products and services you offer.

The IOM definition includes the word 'anticipating', and this is also important, as customers' requirements change over time. For example, in many parts of the world, due mainly to declining birth rates, the average age of the population is rising. This suggests that the demand for products and services for the elderly (e.g. spectacles, sheltered housing) in such areas is likely to increase, while the demand for products and services for young people (e.g. toys, schools) may fall. The long-time survival of a business may depend on its anticipating trends such as these and adapting to them.

The marketing approach emphasises that the most important ingredient of any business is its customers. Marketing is therefore much more than just a function within an organisation. It is a way of thinking, an approach or attitude which should pervade every aspect of a business, from purchasing and production to sales and distribution. Marketing is therefore just as essential to the small businessman as to the multi-national corporation. What's more, because the small businessman is usually in close personal contact with his customers, he has a marketing advantage over larger competitors which can often be exploited.

Marketing is described in the IOM definition as a management process, and this is especially relevant where the business employs one or more staff. There is little value in a proprietor becoming marketing-aware if his employees, who deal with customers on a day-to-day basis, couldn't give a damn. In marketing-led organisations, every operation is directed towards identifying customers' needs and fulfilling them. In such organisations, staff training and management constantly inculcate the message that 'In this business the customer is King.'

However, it should also be said that becoming a business with 'the marketing outlook' does not mean trying to be all things to all people. The IOM definition includes one other key word, 'profitably'. In other words, as well as identifying or anticipating a requirement and then satisfying it, you must be able to make a reasonable profit by doing so.

THE MARKETING MIX

I have already said that marketing is a process which should extend through every aspect of a business, from production, through advertising, to delivery of the product to the customer, and beyond. This process is sometimes referred to as the marketing mix. A popular model used to describe this is the Four Ps: Product, Price, Place and Promotion.

Product

This is the actual product or service you are selling. The category includes such things as design, appearance, technical features, quality, reliability, brand name, packaging, etc. As I noted earlier, it is a mistake to think that you can sell anything by advertising. The marketing approach emphasises researching what customers want, then setting out to provide it. In particular, it is important to find out the benefits your customers want, then ensure that your product or service provides them.

Price

This includes not only specific prices, but also any discounts, easy payment terms, trade-in allowances (where you accept an item from the customer in part-payment of your bill), and so on. Pricing is of course partly an economic decision - the price you charge must in most cases cover all your costs and make a contribution towards your profits. Beyond this, however, pricing is a marketing factor, and will be influenced by such things as what your competitors charge, the selling prices recommended by manufacturers or suppliers, and what you consider is the best price to charge to generate the largest profits (selling a large number of items at a low price may be more profitable than selling a small number at a higher price).

Psychological factors can also come into play. One common marketing technique is to price just below a certain whole figure, e.g. £1.99 or £99. These prices look much cheaper, at first glance anyway, than £2.00 or £100. On the other hand, there are dangers in goods appearing too cheap, especially if quality is one of the main benefits you are offering. People expect to pay a reasonable price for good products, and may be suspicious if your 'quality' goods are priced too cheaply.

Place

This relates to how products are transported from the producer to the end-user. Some businesses sell to wholesalers, who sell to retailers, who in turn finally sell to the actual consumers. Others sell direct to the public, perhaps via mail order advertising. Different methods are appropriate to different businesses, and every business must decide the most appropriate channel of distribution for itself.

Place also relates to matters such as location and premises, and the number of competing businesses in the area. For retail businesses in particular, having the right location is crucial. A main road shop will do more trade than one on a side street, even if it is only half the size. It is therefore better to have a small shop on a main road than a larger one on a side street - and even better to have a shop on the corner of two main roads! This is the reason you will almost never see a department store or branch of a multiple shop on a side street. They are always on the main road, where thousands of people pass by every week. The store directors know it is worth paying the extra rent to secure a prime position.

Promotion

This is the activity which communicates knowledge of the product or service to its target customers by means of press advertising, personal selling, public relations, sales promotions, and so on.

The Four Ps provides a useful overview of the marketing mix, but some would argue that it is too simplified. The author Frank Jefkins, in his books such as Modern Marketing, proposes a model containing twenty elements:

1. Conception, invention, innovation or modification of product or service (including research and development).
2. Product life-cycle.
3. Marketing research.
4. Naming and branding.
5. Product image.
6. Market segment.
7. Pricing.
8. Product mix, rationalisation and standardisation.
9. Packaging.
10. Distribution.
11. Sales force.
12. Market education.
13. Corporate and financial public relations (PR).
14. Industrial relations.
15. Test marketing.
16. Advertising.
17. Advertising research.
18. Sales promotion.

19. The after-market.
20. Maintaining customer interest and loyalty.

While Jefkins' model may be rather too complex and detailed to be much use to the average small businessman, it does clearly demonstrate that the marketing mix is an ongoing process, beginning with the creation of a new product or service, going through to selling to customers, and beyond.

'Doing business without advertising is like winking at a girl in the dark. You know what you're doing but no-one else does.'

Stewart H. Britt - American advertising consultant

ADVERTISING AND THE MARKETING MIX
What is the purpose of advertising? A simple definition is 'persuasive communication'. Advertising aims to bring a product or service to the attention of potential customers, and persuade them - or start to persuade them - to buy. When spending money on advertising, you aim to recover your advertising costs and more - hopefully much more - from increased sales. Advertising is not a precise science, however, and results can never be guaranteed.

DOES EVERY BUSINESS HAVE TO ADVERTISE?
The alternative to advertising is to rely on word-of-mouth and personal recommendations to provide fresh customers. For some self-employed people this may be quite sufficient. Some financial advisers, for example, obtain new clients entirely through recommendations from existing ones. This can be a very effective - and cheap - way of generating new business. Another example might be a self-employed builder who has enough work ahead to keep him occupied for the next twelve months. There is little point in him advertising (now), because he will be unable to start any new jobs until the end of that time.

In general, if you have enough customers coming to you by word-of-mouth and personal recommendation, there is little point in advertising. Most businesses, however, will need to advertise at least some of the time.

WHY YOU NEED AN ADVERTISING STRATEGY
If you do decide to advertise to generate sales, you should have some kind of plan or strategy to guide you. The aim of your advertising strategy should be to bring potential customers from a state of ignorance about your product or service to a desire to purchase it. The practical side to this is discussed in the next chapter. Your advertising should:

- Get customers' attention.
- Help them understand the product or service.
- Get them to believe in the benefits you are offering.
- Make them want to buy your product or service.
- Get them to take action (e.g. fill in a coupon or make a phone call).
- Improve the business's image and reputation.

No one advertisement on its own can be expected to achieve all this. Rather, you will need to use a mixture of forms of advertising over a period of time. This point is particularly important. It is easy to believe, if you have taken out a half-page advertisement in your local paper, that everybody in the area now knows about your business. This is a mistake. People forget about adverts almost as soon as they have read them, unless they happen to need your product or service at that particular moment. It is therefore very important, if you are going to use advertising, to advertise regularly.

Regular advertising has other benefits as well. For one thing, if an individual sees your advertisement every week or month, your name is more likely to come into his mind should he at some point have need of your services. For another, if you advertise regularly, people will, in general, be more inclined to see your business as established and reliable, and unlikely to disappear overnight with their money. This is one reason you will sometimes see businesses advertising 'established 1954' (or whatever). It all helps give an impression of stability and reliability.

On the other hand, it must be said that in some types of business, regular advertising may cause a degree of suspicion among potential customers. Tradesmen such as builders and plumbers, for example, tend to obtain much of their work through word-of-mouth recommendation from satisfied customers. If such individuals advertise regularly, some people may conclude that if they need to advertise that much they cannot be very good! It is difficult to give hard-and-fast advice about this, as so much depends on local factors (e.g. are there many other businesses in the area offering this service, or just a few?). The best advice is to put yourself in the place of a potential customer. If you saw a business such as yours advertising every week, would you be impressed by this or suspicious about it?

Where can you advertise?
There is a huge range of choice when it comes to deciding where (and how) you will advertise. Some of the possibilities include:

- Local and national newspapers.
- Consumer and trade magazines.

- TV and radio.
- Cinema.
- Directories and Yearbooks.
- Handbills.
- Brochures/inserts.
- Advertising cards.
- Posters.
- Direct mail.
- The Internet
- Exhibitions.
- Buses and coaches.
- Theatre and sports programmes.
- Point-of-sale material.
- Packaging.
- Newsagents' windows.
...and more!

With such a wide choice available, it is important to devote careful thought to your choice of advertising media. As we will see in the next chapter, the crucial thing here is your target market segment - the people you want to sell to. For example, if you are running a car repair service and your target segment is car owners within a five mile radius, there would be no point in advertising in a national, or even a regional, newspaper. Many of the people reading your advertisement would be outside your target area, and so unlikely, or unable, to use your services.

Cost is a major consideration here. Small businesses have limited marketing budgets, and need to spend them as effectively as possible. If your business serves just your local community, there is little point spending money sending your message to other parts of the country; the local newspaper may therefore be your best choice.

On the other hand, if you are selling a hobby item by mail order to customers all over the UK, you need a medium which reaches as many people as possible who pursue this hobby. A special interest magazine may then be the best option.

'The philosophy behind much advertising is based on the old observation that every man is really two men - the man he is and the man he wants to be.'

William Feather - American businessman

POSITIONING
As well as the advertising medium you choose, your target market segment will also help determine what form your advertising

should take. This is known as positioning. If, for example, you are aiming at an upper-middle class market segment with high disposable incomes, the general appearance of your advertising will need to match the lifestyle and expectations of this group. Even the layout and typeface must be chosen to help project the desired sense of luxury and opulence.

ADVERTISING AGENCIES

Most small businesses start out by handling their own advertising, but at some point many consider employing an agency. Using an agency has the obvious advantage that the agency staff are designing advertisements every day of the week, so they should be able to come up with better ideas than the average new small business. They will also have extensive experience and expertise in areas such as design, artwork and print buying.

The main drawback of using an agency is, of course, the cost. Advertising agencies receive commission from the publications or TV/radio stations in which they place their clients' advertising, so this helps to offset their charges. Nevertheless, agencies do not come cheap, and there will still be fees to pay. (Of course, an agency's fees must be viewed in the light of the extra sales their advertisements generate for you.)

For small businesses whose advertising amounts to no more than the occasional classified ad in their local paper, an advertising agency is unlikely to be required. If you intend to advertise more widely, however - and especially if you are planning to advertise regionally or nationally - using the services of an advertising agency is worth considering.

An agency will first advise you on your advertising policy in general. They will design and write your advertisements for you, and book space for them in the appropriate media. Agencies will also produce and book advertisements for TV or radio where required. Most agencies will also assist with other types of publicity such as press releases and publicity brochures.

If you decide to engage an advertising agency, remember that - like banks, solicitors and accountants - they are in competition with one another for your custom. Therefore, don't be in too much of a hurry to make a decision. Arrange to visit at least three different agencies. The largest agencies are probably not worth approaching, as they are unlikely to want to take on new small businesses.

Seek out new - but not too new - agencies which are actively looking to expand their client base. Take along samples of your product and any advertising material you have already produced, and listen to what they say. Ask to see samples of their previous work. You should look for an agency which understands and has some experience of your product or service, and with whose staff you, personally, feel some rapport.

THE LIMITS OF ADVERTISING

I would like to conclude this chapter with a reminder and a warning: no advertising, however expensive or sophisticated, can sell a fundamentally sub-standard product (except, perhaps, once). Advertising is an important part of the marketing mix, but unless it supports a good product or service, it will be so much wasted effort.

KEY POINTS

- Advertising needs to be seen as just one aspect of marketing. This is a process which involves identifying and anticipating customer requirements, and satisfying them profitably.
- The marketing mix is a model which is often used to explain the marketing process. One simple version includes four elements: Product, Price, Place and Promotion.
- A more complex model containing twenty elements was provided by Frank Jefkins. Jefkins' model makes very clear that marketing is a process running through every aspect of a business, from new product creation to customer sales and after-care.
- Advertising is persuasive communication. It aims to bring a product or service to the attention of potential customers, and persuade them - or start to persuade them - to buy.
- Not all businesses advertise. Where word-of-mouth alone brings in sufficient customers, there is little point spending money on advertising. The same applies if you are unable to take on any more business for a lengthy period.
- If you do decide to advertise, you should have clear aims and objectives.
- Advertising is usually most effective if it is continuous over a period of weeks or months.
- Regular advertising also helps give the impression that your business is well-established and reliable.
- There is a huge range of places you can advertise. Your choice will depend largely on which medium offers the most cost-effective way of communicating with people in your target market segment.
- Your target market segment will also influence the form which your advertisement should take (positioning).
- Advertising agencies are businesses which will assist you with your advertising. They recoup part of their fees in the form of commission from publications in which they place advertisements.
- For very small businesses an advertising agency may not be worthwhile, but they should be considered when planning a national or regional campaign.

- Advertising has its limits. No advertising can sell a product which is basically sub-standard.

CHAPTER TWO

YOUR ADVERTISING STRATEGY

The first principle of advertising is that you should know why you want to advertise. Contrary to what you might at first think, there is a wide range of possible reasons. They include:

- Opening new premises.
- Launching a new product.
- Attending an exhibition.
- Recruiting new staff.
- Inviting enquiries (direct response advertising).
- Selling 'off the page'.
- Reminding customers you are still there.
- Appealing for agents.
- Publicising a special offer.
- Ironing out seasonal variations in demand.

As mentioned in the last chapter, in some circumstances (e.g. where word of mouth alone brings in sufficient business) advertising may not be necessary. 'Because Billy down the road does it' is not, in itself, a good reason for doing likewise.

ADVERTISING TO SELL
The most common reason for advertising is, directly or indirectly, to sell more of your products (or services). Advertising provides

the method by which you can bring your product to the attention of potential customers, and persuade them - or start to persuade them - to buy.

To be effective, advertising needs to be carefully planned. An essential preliminary to this is to find out as much as possible about your current and potential customers. You need to know the answers to such questions as:

- Who and where are our existing customers?
- What is it about our product that makes them buy it?
- Why do they come to us rather than our competitors?
- Who and where are our potential customers?
- What would it take to persuade them to come to us?
- What are the best channels to reach existing and potential customers through our advertising?

To answer these and similar questions fully, we need to start by addressing the most fundamental question of all...

WHY DO PEOPLE BUY?

The obvious answer to this question is to obtain the product or service concerned; but this ignores the fact that people could (in most cases) just as easily buy from a competitor. So what are the reasons which make a customer buy one particular product from one particular supplier?

One of the most important is, of course, price. Other things being equal, if the same product is available at a lower price from supplier A than supplier B, the customer will go to A every time. Even with highly price-sensitive products such as petrol, however, other considerations are frequently operating as well.

For example, with the petrol purchaser an equally important factor may be convenience (is the petrol station on his usual route to work?). Indeed, if the petrol is paid for by his employer, convenience may be much more important to him. With a little thought, you will soon see that customers may have a wide range of reasons for buying. Other than price, they may include:

- Appearance (including colour, shape, design, etc.).
- Reliability.
- Quality.
- Performance.
- Delivery time.
- Safety.
- Reputation/recommendation of others.
- Convenience.
- Habit.
.....and more!

For your advertising to be effective, you need to know what are the most important considerations for your customers - existing and potential - in deciding what to buy. If, for example, your reputation for quality is a major factor in bringing customers to you, advertising which emphasises the low cost of your services could have the opposite effect from what you intended, by implying to people that you are going 'down market'.

On the other hand, if price is a major factor in determining where customers buy, you emphasise other things at your peril. An example from my own experience concerns motor insurance. Earlier this year I received my renewal forms, and noticed that the premium was higher than I had paid last year. I phoned round and obtained a lower price from another broker, which I accepted. It was only when writing to my former insurers telling them that I had made alternative arrangements I noticed in the small print that the price they had quoted included optional extras such as free car hire in the event of an accident.

Had I not wanted these (which, as I don't intend to have an accident, I didn't), I could have deducted £20 from the price, making it cheaper than the quote I actually took up. The result was that my original brokers lost my business, now and in the future, simply because they failed to appreciate that by far the most important feature I was looking for in motor insurance was low cost. A further consideration to take into account is that the reasons people have for buying one product rather than another are not always the obvious, logical ones. Sometimes, even in trade and industrial markets, emotional factors come into play as well. These include such things as:

- Wanting to be liked.
- Wanting to appear stylish.
- Wanting to appear decisive.
- Wanting to appear fashionable.
- Wanting to be different.
- Wanting to conform.

Much of this comes down to one word - image. People buy a product or service not simply for its features, but for the image which goes with it. Ford cars, for example, have a safe, traditional image, while the image associated with Porsche is glamorous and exciting. People like to buy into a product which complements the image they have of themselves. If you are aiming to sell to young, professional people, for example, you may wish to present an image that is dynamic and thrusting. On the other hand, if you are aiming at older people, a friendly, traditional image may be more appropriate. Once you have a picture in your mind of the kind of people you hope to sell to, you will be much better placed to target your advertising at them.

> *'All things being equal, people will buy from a friend. All things being not quite so equal, people will still buy from a friend.'*

Mark McCormack - Chairman of International Management Group

FEATURES, BENEFITS AND USPs

We have seen that people may have any of a wide range of reasons for buying from one particular supplier. In general, however, products are bought because of the benefits customers think they will obtain from their purchase. Effective advertising therefore highlights the benefits obtainable through owning or using a product - rather than the product's features, which are mainly of interest to the manufacturer.

This is an important distinction, and worth emphasising. Features are things you incorporate in your product or service, such as energy-saving controls or a five-year guarantee; benefits are the advantages which accrue for the customer as a result (lower power bills, added peace of mind). It is the benefits they will receive, rather than the features you include, which will be foremost in customers' minds when they are deciding what to buy.

Furthermore, it is the benefits you offer, compared with your competitors, which determine whether customers will decide to buy from you. It is therefore essential to find out what benefits customers want, so that you can build the appropriate features into your product or service. Your advertising will then spell out the benefits which the customer will enjoy when he purchases from you.

A Unique Selling Proposition (USP) is a piece of ad-man's jargon which has passed into common usage. A USP is simply a feature which no other supplier offers. A USP is by no means essential to running a successful business, but if you have one it may be worth emphasising in your advertising ('Last Chance To Fill Up Before the Border', 'The only genuine Belgian restaurant in Middletown!'). However, as with all benefits, it is important to be sure that your USP really does represent something which customers will find attractive.

YOUR TARGET MARKET SEGMENT

So far we have mainly been concerned with why customers buy, but now we need to look in a little more detail at who these customers might be. As we noted in the last chapter, it is usually a mistake to aim your advertising at too wide a target audience. For most small businesses, a better strategy is to find a niche or segment which you can serve profitably. Segments are groups of people with something in common. Once you have identified a particular market segment (or segments) as your potential customers, you can start preparing your strategy for turning these people from potential into actual customers.

There are many ways of segmenting markets, and it is up to you to decide which might be most relevant for your business. Some of the most common methods are listed below.

By geographical location
This will be relevant for many small businesses serving a local community. You might decide to segment the market into potential customers living within (say) a 3 mile radius, a 5 mile radius and a 10 mile radius. For many products and services people prefer to shop locally if they can, as this saves them time, effort and travel costs.

By age
You could segment the market into children, teenagers, young adults, parents, middle-aged people and older people. Each of these groups might have different requirements. If you run a hairdresser's shop, for instance, you may need different approaches according to whether you wish to appeal to young, fashion-conscious people or to older people with more traditional needs.

By sex
You could simply divide potential customers into male and female. This will be more relevant for some businesses than others - but even in the case of products and services used by both sexes it may be useful to segment the market in this way. For example, men wanting to use a taxi service might rate speed and value for money as the most important qualities they were looking for, while women might put personal security as their top priority. This difference is not just of theoretical interest. Some taxi services have been set up in cities serving women exclusively, addressing their wish for a secure, reliable service. Their proprietors decided to launch businesses specifically aimed at meeting the needs of this particular market segment.

By type of customer
There are many ways of segmenting the market by type of customer. One of the most important is between trade and private customers. A major difference here is that trade customers

will expect credit - anything from a week to 30 days, sometimes as much as 90 days - whereas private customers will usually pay immediately or make their own arrangement with a finance company (unless you also offer credit facilities, of course). Trade customers generally have a larger budget, but the fact that they expect credit needs to be taken into account in your cash flow. Another area in which trade customers differ from the general public is that it is frequently not their own money they are spending. They are therefore more likely to be concerned about matters such as reliability, quality of service, workmanship and so on, and (relatively) less concerned about price.

Another form of segmentation according to type of customer is by social class. This is discussed in more detail in the next chapter. Some products and services may appeal more to members of one social class than another, and this can be relevant when you are trying to sell to a particular segment. For example, an office caterer providing food and drinks for a predominantly middle-class workforce might need to offer quite a different range of products from a mobile snack bar in the middle of a factory estate. To repeat the main point, the purpose of segmenting the market is to find one or more groups or market segments who will be your potential customers. You will then be able to plan every aspect of your advertising with these people in mind.

CHOOSING YOUR TARGET MARKET

To be attractive to a business, a market segment should ideally have the following qualities:

- Enough people in it to make serving the segment profitable.
- The segment is growing, or at least stable, rather than shrinking.
- There are unsatisfied needs among this group of people which the business could profitably meet.
- There is not so much competition among existing firms that another operator would be unable to attract a sufficient share of the market.

You will need to do some research to find out the size, level of competition, and profit potential of particular segments. Having completed the research, and clarified the make-up of your chosen groups, you then face a choice. You can do one of the following:

1. Ignore the differences between segments and try to develop a product or service which concentrates on meeting the needs of a wide range of potential customers.
2. Recognise the differing needs of people in different market

segments, and try to offer a range of products or services tailored to meet as many as possible of these.

3. Recognise the differing needs of people in different market segments, but choose to offer a narrow range of products or services concentrated on no more than a small number of chosen groups.

None of these strategies is necessarily better than any other, and each may be appropriate at a different stage in a business's development. For small businesses, however, 3 is often the best strategy for gaining a foothold in the market, so long as there are sufficient potential customers in that particular market segment.

'He who has a thing to sell goes and whispers in a well, is not so apt to get the dollars as he who climbs a tree and hollers.'

Anon

MARKET RESEARCH

The foregoing was intended to make you aware of how important it is to understand your customer: not only why he buys (or is going to buy) your product, but when, where and how as well.

Some of these questions you may be able to answer from your own experience, or by asking friends and colleagues. To get a more accurate picture, however, you may need to do some practical market research. If at all possible, you will need to speak to existing and potential customers, to find out what exactly they want from your product or service, and what influences them when they are deciding what to choose.

If you sell through retailers (or wholesalers), you can approach them for help and advice. They will have a good knowledge of what their customers want, and will not mind sharing this information with you. After all, if your product sells well, their profits will increase also.

If you sell direct to the public, the option above will not be open to you. Instead, you will need to research customers directly. A popular way of doing this is by enclosing a short questionnaire with your product - or handing one to customers after providing your service - and giving some incentive to complete and return it (e.g. entry in a free prize draw). Of course, this only works with existing rather than potential customers, and it is not an option available for new businesses who are not yet trading.

To get the views of potential customers, you will need to find some way of identifying such people, and persuade them to spend a few minutes answering some questions. If your customers will be other businesses, you could try going round a local industrial estate, or phoning up a few relevant companies in Yellow Pages. If you will be selling direct to the public, you could literally stop people in the street, or go round from door to door. However you do this, it is a good idea to have a standard set of questions - a questionnaire - to ask. Asking everyone the same questions will give you a good idea of the relative importance of different influences on buying.

For example, if everyone you speak to mentions quality or reliability as a major factor in determining where they purchase your particular service, you will know that this should be a good benefit to offer and emphasise in your advertising.

DESIGNING A QUESTIONNAIRE

A questionnaire is simply a list of questions which you either fill in yourself or ask your subject to complete. The following are a few basic principles to follow when designing one.

Keep it short and simple

Most people will not object to answering a few simple questions, but a multi-page document which will take up hours of their time is a different matter. Think carefully about what you need to find out, and ask only the most important things. There should be no more than five to ten questions in total. Wherever possible use yes/no questions and multiple choice (where the person answering has to choose from a list of possible answers), as these are both easier to complete and to understand.

Don't ask 'loaded' questions

A loaded question is one which invites a particular answer. If, for instance, you ask, 'Would you use my service if it was cheaper than all the other ones', most people will answer 'Yes' without much thought. It is better to ask neutral, factual questions such as, 'Where do you buy your groceries at present?' or 'How many times this year have you used a taxi service?' The information you obtain from questions such as these will be much more useful to you.

Don't ask too many 'open' questions

All questions can be either open or closed. A closed question allows only a limited number of replies - two in the case of yes/no questions, perhaps half a dozen with multiple choice. This makes closed questions quick and easy to answer. By contrast, open questions (such as, "What do you think of a mobile car repair service?") allow a huge range of possible answers.

Occasionally open questions may produce interesting and unexpected replies which can affect your whole thinking about your advertising and your business generally. But they can also lead to lengthy discussion and debate, and replies to them can be very difficult to compare and analyse. For that reason, it is normally best to have no more than one or two open questions on your questionnaire.

Ask the right people

There is no point in talking to people who are not potential customers. As already mentioned, finding the right people may require house-to-house interviews or stopping people in the street. It will also depend on the type of business you plan to start. For example, if you are intend to start a printing service, you will need to talk to people in local small businesses who are likely to be your main clients.

Ask as many people as you can

The more people you interview, the more useful and accurate your results are likely to be. Rather than try to cram all your answers on to one piece of paper, it is a good idea to make photocopies of your questionnaire and complete one for every person you ask. This makes adding up the figures at the end much easier.

POSTAL SURVEYS

Interviewing people, whether in the street, in their homes or in businesses, can be difficult and very time-consuming. A possible alternative is to conduct a postal survey. This involves writing to a number of potential customers with a list of questions and some means of returning it to you with their answers. Postal surveys are simple to do and relatively inexpensive. However:

1. Many people who receive the questionnaire may not bother to complete it.
2. Some people may reply flippantly, or deliberately attempt to deceive you. This is much harder to detect in postal surveys where no interviewer is physically present.
3. It is likely to be predominantly people with a particular interest in your product or service who bother to reply; this means you could get a distorted view of the market as a whole.

To get the best response, postal questionnaires need to be kept short and simple. Try to make them as interesting and entertaining as you can! Wherever possible, give respondents boxes to tick rather than forcing them to write out their answers.

A reply-paid envelope makes returning the questionnaire less trouble and ensures that respondents are not out of pocket. You could also increase the likelihood of a good response by mentioning that all completed questionnaires will be entered into a free prize draw (which you will, of course, have - the prize is a legitimate business expense!).

INFORMAL RESEARCH

Although surveys using questionnaires are the ideal way to find out about potential customers, using them may sometimes present practical difficulties. However there are many less formal ways of researching your market such as:

- Talking to family members, friends and workmates.
- Talking to people already in similar businesses (especially in other areas, with whom you will not be competing directly).
- Observing similar businesses.
- Using your own personal judgement: what would you want if you were a potential customer?

Informal market research can take many different forms, and allows considerable scope for ingenuity. Wherever possible, however, it should be accompanied by more formal research using questionnaires.

OTHER INFLUENCES ON BUYING

There are various factors influencing people's buying which you may need to investigate in your market research. As well as what they are looking for in a product or service, they include:

When do they buy?

Some products are bought all the year round, while others sell more at some times of the year than others. Sales of goods which are bought mainly as gifts, for example, peak around Christmas, while goods such as sun lotion and many garden products sell best in the summer. Some products such as cars may be bought only once every few years, while others such as bread and milk may be bought several times a week.

Whom are they buying for?

Are customers buying for themselves, for an employer, or for friends and relatives? The type of benefits they are seeking may be different in each case. For example, price may not be as important a consideration when buying gifts as it might be when buying for yourself. People buying for an employer may be more cautious, and hence more influenced by factors such as a product's reputation, than they would be when buying for themselves.

How do they buy?

As well as the motivation for buying, customers must have the means to pay. Low-cost goods and services are usually paid for in cash, but more expensive purchases may be bought with the aid of a loan. The loan may be obtained separately by the customer (e.g. from a bank or credit card), or credit facilities may be offered by the supplier. Your research needs to establish how customers may wish to pay, and as far as possible ensure that you are able to accommodate their wishes.

Where do they buy?

Nowadays people have a huge range of choices about where they buy a product. The possibilities include local shops, supermarkets, the nearest town or city, out-of-town shopping centres, street markets, and so on. In addition, there is an increasing number of new methods of buying, such as party plan, mail order catalogues, direct response, telemarketing, interactive shopping via TV screen/computer, vending machines, and so on. Many products are, of course, most commonly sold through shops, and if you intend to make a product which falls into this category you will probably need to do likewise. There are broadly three main types of product which sell through shops, and each requires a different approach to advertising.

1. Shopping goods are those where the customer typically shops around, comparing items and prices in a number of different places. Examples might include kitchen-ware, electric shavers, clothes, DIY products etc.
2. Convenience goods, also known as fast-moving consumer goods (FMCGs), are staple goods such as milk, bread and vegetables found in every supermarket. They are bought frequently, often according to habit, and with little consideration of alternatives.
3. Speciality or durable goods are more expensive items bought only occasionally, such as cars, cameras and CD players. Considerable care and effort is devoted to making the right choice.

MEDIA SELECTION

Having completed your research, you should have a good idea of who your existing and potential customers are, and what they are looking for in your product or service. You will now be in a much better position to decide where you need to advertise to reach them. This is the area of media selection - something I touched on in the last chapter, but must now cover in more detail.

In this section I will be dealing mainly with print advertising, as this is the type of advertising small businesses make most use of. Printed publications deliver the largest audience at the lowest cost per head, and are generally accepted as the best way for a small business to reach a mass audience. This is made easier by the fact that there is a huge range of publications serving every conceivable occupation, interest and geographical area. However, the principles described in this section apply equally well to other advertising media.

MAKING A START

One obvious starting point in choosing where to advertise is your own knowledge and experience. If you are providing a service to people in the area where you live, you are likely to have a good idea which media they are most likely to see. In my town, for example, there are at least three local papers, but only one of these (which has the best editorial coverage) is widely read by local people. This is the paper I would use if I were advertising a business in the area - and, judging by the fact that it contains more advertising than the other two papers put together, it is clear that many local businesses agree with me. Indeed, if there is any uncertainty in your mind about where to advertise, checking where other, similar businesses advertise can provide a useful pointer.

If you are selling to a more dispersed market - perhaps to other traders and retailers, or by mail order to people with a special interest or hobby - finding the best way of reaching them can be less clear-cut. Again, your own knowledge and experience should stand you in good stead, but you should be prepared to do some research to find out the possible advertising media.

The most useful source of information on titles covering your area of activity is BRAD (British Rate And Data), the so-called Advertisers' Bible. This is a comprehensive list of around 12,000 UK publications, including:

- National newspapers.
- Regional newspapers.
- Free newspapers (freesheets).
- Weeklies.
- Consumer magazines.
- Trade and technical magazines.
- Business journals and newsletters.

The information in BRAD includes:

- The publications' names, addresses and phone/fax numbers.
- The types of advertising they accept and what they charge.

- A breakdown of their circulation (subscriptions, copies sold through newsagents, copies distributed free, and so on).
- Technical specifications (including page size, publication dates, when advertisements must be submitted, and so on).

BRAD is updated monthly, and you can buy an annual subscription or a single copy.

Their address is: 33-39 Bowling Green Lane, London, EC1R 0DA, tel. 020 7505 8000. BRAD is expensive to buy - at the time of writing a year's subscription costs £495, a single copy £260 - but slightly out of date copies can be bought from the publishers at reduced prices. Some large libraries keep a copy, or you might be able to beg or borrow an old one from your local advertising agency.

If you are not successful in tracking down a copy of BRAD, you could obtain a media directory such as Willings Press Guide or Benn's Media Directory. These do not have such detailed information about advertising costs and circulation, but will at least alert you to the range of publications serving your area of interest. Begin by identifying all of the publications which may cover your target market (existing and potential customers). Contact all these publications explaining that you are a potential advertiser, and ask for a sample copy (if you haven't already seen the publication) and a copy of their rate card. The latter covers advertising costs and circulation, and often comes with additional information on the readership of the publication.

CIRCULATION AND READERSHIP

Circulation is the number of copies of a newspaper or magazine which are distributed. Most publications have their circulations independently certified by the ABC (Audit Bureau of Circulation), and the figures quoted are generally accurate. Smaller journals may not belong to the ABC scheme, and the word 'Uncertified' will appear beside their circulation figures in BRAD. Any figure quoted will have been supplied by the publisher, and should obviously not be taken as gospel.

Other things being equal, you will obviously wish to advertise in a magazine which has as large a circulation as possible. A useful, if crude, method of comparing the cost of advertising in different publications is the cost per thousand (CPT). This is calculated by dividing the cost of advertising per page by the total circulation, and multiplying by a thousand. For example, if advertising costs £600 per page, and the total circulation is 120,000, then the cost per thousand is:

$$(600/120,000) \times 1000 = £5 \text{ per thousand}$$

The CPT provides a rough and ready way of comparing advertising costs, but it has its limitations. For one thing, the circulation figures do not reveal the total number of people who actually read the publication. Readership is always larger than circulation. (The classic example is Reader's Digest, old copies of which have a huge readership in doctors' and dentists' waiting rooms.)

Readership is obviously impossible to estimate accurately, but advertising sales people will be quick to tell you of the large numbers of readers who peruse each copy of their publication. Common sense needs to be applied here. In general, most consumer magazines have a fairly small readership: the purchaser and maybe one or two members of his family. Trade and technical magazines tend to have a higher readership per copy, as do business journals. Free publications may have huge circulations, but many are sent unsolicited and may be binned without even being opened. Their average readership may even be less than one per copy.

READERSHIP PROFILES

As well as their number, you need to know something about the readers themselves. Many advertisers provide a wide range of information here, including the numbers of readers in different age groups, the ratio of male to female, and so on. Another widely used method of describing readership is socio-economic. This divides up the population as follows:

A : Upper middle class – Higher professional, administrative or managerial.
B : Middle class – Intermediate professional, administrative or managerial.
C1 : Lower middle class – Supervisory or clerical; junior managerial, administrative or professional.
C2 : Skilled working class – Skilled manual workers.
D : Working class – Semi-skilled and unskilled manual workers.
E : People at the lowest level of subsistence – The un-employed, people on basic state pensions, casual workers.

Whatever you may think of these divisions, they can provide you with some useful information when comparing the readership of different publications. People in social classes A and B, for example, are likely to have the highest disposable incomes, and may be the type of people you most wish to reach if you are selling luxury items such as boats or caravans. On the other hand, if you are offering correspondence courses or business opportunity plans, classes C1 and C2 may be the most receptive to your advertising.

COVERAGE

A final consideration is the extent to which any particular publication will reach your target market segment. This is known as the penetration or coverage. It is difficult to estimate accurately, though some publications will provide an analysis showing, for example, the proportion of all women between the ages of 18 and 25 who read the publication.

A complicating factor is that in any given field there is always a certain amount of duplication - people who read more than one publication. Thus, if you advertise in one magazine there may be little point in advertising in its rival if most people in your target market segment read both. Accurate information is obviously hard to come by here. However, in the area of trade and professional magazines in particular, a useful tactic can be to phone up a few potential customers and ask them which publications they read themselves. This can be quite an eye-opener.

In some fields there is a widely respected professional journal to which everyone pays lip service, but also a more popular and accessible one which people read when they really want to know what is going on in their field. The latter may well be more effective as an advertising medium.

TYPE OF BUSINESS	% OF SALES INCOME USED FOR ADVERTISING
Food	0.95%
Clothing	0.35%
Drink/tobacco	1.12%
Automotive	0.69%
Medical/toiletries	5.96%
Household/Leisure	1.61%
Publishing	2.05%
Tourism/Entertainment	0.75%
Retail	0.49%
Financial/Savings	0.63%
Industrial	0.47%

Source: The Advertising Association

BUDGETING

Having researched the available media and discovered which should be best for reaching your target market segment, you now face the task of deciding how much money you should spend on advertising. The bad news is, there is no foolproof, scientific method for calculating this. Even many large companies use methods of budgeting which could fairly be described as arbitrary.

One useful way of looking at advertising expenditure is to compare it against sales. Some published statistics are available here. The chart above shows the average percentage of advertising expenditure compared with sales over eight years in 11 different business sectors.

You will see from the table that the proportion of sales income spent on advertising varies between sectors, but a figure of about 1% is fairly typical. This can provide a useful starting point in working out your own advertising budget. For example, if your total gross annual income from sales is £300,000 (or, in the case of a new business, this is the figure you are aiming for), spending 1% of this on advertising would give you a budget of £3,000 a year. This is a widely-accepted method of deciding advertising budgets; but before deciding on the final figure a range of other factors must also be taken into account.

1. If the product you are selling has a high mark-up/profit margin, you will be able to spend a higher proportion of your sales income on advertising while still leaving enough profit to make the business successful.
2. Conversely, if you are selling something with a low mark-up, you will need to limit your advertising budget more severely. Taking this to (admittedly ridiculous) extremes, if your profit margin is 1% and the advertising budget is 1% of sales income, then all your profits will be going on advertising.
3. In markets where the customer buys only one of a product at lengthy intervals (e.g. cars), you will need to advertise more frequently to attract new customers. On the other hand, if the same customers keep coming back regularly (e.g. window cleaning) you may not need to spend much on advertising at all.
4. If you are trading in a fast-changing market where new products are constantly coming on to the market (e.g. computers), you will need to spend more on advertising to remain visible.
5. If you are selling a commonplace product you are likely to have to spend more money to get it noticed and accepted. Conversely, if you are providing an unusual, specialist service, especially if there is little other competition, you may not need to spend much on advertising.

6. With a new and innovative product or service, you may need to spend a larger proportion of your budget on public relations to inform and educate people about it, and to take full advantage of its newsworthiness. Once this phase has passed, you may need to switch some of your promotional budget from PR to advertising.

However much you decide to spend on advertising, it is important to plan ahead for a specific period, say six months or a year. The money need not be allocated equally for each month. For example, with products where demand is seasonal you may find it appropriate to budget more at certain times of year to try to even out demand. If you are planning a new product launch, or to exhibit at a prestigious conference, you may need to allocate additional funding around those times.

Regularly monitor how your advertising spending compares with the amounts set out in the budget, not forgetting to include an amount for overheads such as postage, phone calls, photocopying. Be prepared to make adjustments to your budget if this seems appropriate, perhaps increasing or decreasing expenditure in line with sales. Budgets should be used to assist in determining spending, not dictate it.

Finally, if at all possible set aside a reserve which can be used if an unexpected new advertising opportunity presents itself, or if a change in the market necessitates extra advertising (e.g. a new competitor appears on the scene and is advertising aggressively).

To recap, in this and the preceding chapter we have looked at the reasons why you might wish to advertise, and the principles of advertising successfully. If you have followed the suggestions in this chapter, you should now have a good idea of the kind of places where you might wish to advertise, and how much you intend to spend. In the following chapters we will look at the art of creating successful advertisements, and making the most of the opportunities offered by the various advertising media.

KEY POINTS

- You should always have a good reason for advertising. Often this will be to sell more of your product, but there are other possible reasons to advertise as well.
- For your advertising to be effective, you need to know as much about your existing and potential customers as possible.
- People have many reasons for buying from a particular supplier. One is cost, but others include appearance, reliability, quality, performance, delivery time, safety, reputation, convenience and habit.
- It is important to find out what considerations are the most

important for your customers - existing and potential - in deciding what to buy. You can then build these features into your product and highlight them in your advertising.

- Reasons for buying are not always logical. Emotional factors come into play as well. These often revolve around a product's image. To appeal to potential customers, your advertising will need to project an image they find attractive.
- A distinction must be drawn between features and benefits. Features are things put into a product by the manufacturer, while benefits are the advantages which accrue for customers as a result. Good advertising emphasises the benefits of a product rather than its features.
- A USP (Unique Selling Proposition) is a benefit no other supplier offers. A USP is not essential to running a successful business, but if you have one it may be worth emphasising in your advertising. As with all benefits, it is important to be sure that your USP really does represent something customers will find attractive.
- When seeking to attract new customers, it is best to identify a target market segment - a group of people with some characteristics such as age or location in common - and ensure that your advertising reaches these people and appeals to them.
- Small businesses are normally best advised to identify one target market segment initially and concentrate on this. As the business grows, additional market segments can be targeted as well.
- To find out as much as possible about your customers, you will need to do some market research. This will involve contacting customers and asking them questions.
- If you are selling through retailers or wholesalers you can contact them for advice and assistance. They will have a good idea of what sells well to their customers and what doesn't.
- If you are selling to the public, you could try giving customers a short questionnaire to fill in, perhaps with some incentive for completing it such as entry in a free prize draw.
- Questionnaires can also be used with potential customers, so long as you can find some way of identifying them. It is important to locate a group of people who might, in the right circumstances, be interested in buying from you.
- When preparing questionnaires, a few basic principles include: keep them short; avoid 'loaded' questions; don't ask too many 'open' questions; ask the right people; and ask as many as you can.
- A method which can work well in some circumstances is a postal questionnaire, but these have the drawback that response rates may be low and those who do answer may not be typical of customers generally.

- Don't neglect the benefits of informal research. This can include asking friends and family and people running other businesses, and trusting your own 'gut feeling'.
- Other areas worth exploring in your market research include: when people buy, whom they buy for, how they buy, and where they buy. The answers to these questions need to be incorporated into your advertising strategy.
- Most small businesses will spend the major part of their advertising budgets on print advertising, as this is a proven and cost-effective method of reaching a mass audience.
- You will need to research which publications offer the most effective and economical means of reaching your target market segment. In the case of businesses serving their local area, local papers are often best.
- Where the market is more diverse (e.g. if you are selling to people with a particular hobby or interest, or to trade customers) finding the best places to advertise can be more difficult. A useful resource is BRAD (British Rate And Data).
- BRAD lists over 12,000 publications, giving such information as advertising rates, circulation, publication dates and contact details. Other media guides are available, e.g. Benn's and Willings Press Guide, but the information they contain is not as detailed.
- Once you have identified a few potential publications, contact their advertising departments asking for a sample issue and their rate card. The information you receive will often also include information about the readership profile of the publication.
- When comparing different publications, there are various figures to take into account. A magazine's circulation is the number of copies which are actually distributed, while the readership (usually a larger figure) is the number of people who actually read it.
- The cost per thousand (CPT) provides a useful, if crude, method of comparing advertising costs in different publications. It is calculated by dividing the cost of advertising per page by the total circulation, and multiplying by a thousand.
- It is also useful to have some information about the kind of people who read a particular publication. One common method of categorisation is the socio-economic scale. This divides up the population into six groups based on social class.
- You also need to take into account penetration or coverage. This is the extent to which any particular publication reaches your target market segment. A complicating factor is that there can be some duplication of readership, i.e. some people read two or more publications in the same field.

- Budgeting is normally done on the basis of a percentage of total income from sales. A typical figure is around 1%, but this can vary widely between business sectors.
- Other factors to take into account include the profit margin or mark-up on what you are selling - the higher this is, the more you can afford to spend on advertising.
- You must also take into account matters such as whether the market in which you are trading is a fast-moving one, whether you must constantly attract new customers, and so on.
- Budgets need not be allocated evenly over an entire year. It may be appropriate to spend more at certain times of year to counter a seasonal decline in sales, or to take advantage of specific opportunities.
- Monitor all your advertising spending carefully, and be prepared to alter your budget if this seems appropriate.
- If possible, set aside a reserve to take advantage of new advertising opportunities which may arise, or to respond to changing market conditions.
- Remember that, whatever you decide to spend on advertising and wherever you spend it, it must be effective in increasing sales. The need to monitor the performance of all your advertising carefully is a theme returned to in succeeding chapters.

CHAPTER THREE

CLASSIFIED ADVERTISEMENTS

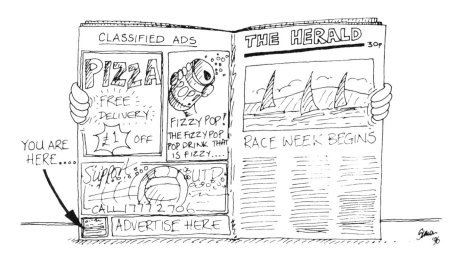

'It is far easier to write ten passably effective sonnets, good enough to take in the not too enquiring critic, than to write one effective advertisement that will take in a few thousand of the buying public.'

Aldous Huxley - British writer

Classified advertisements are the cheapest and simplest form of advertising. At their most basic they consist of two or more lines of text under a specific heading (e.g. builders, car repairs, electrical). You may also have the option of paying extra for 'semi-display' advertising - this is discussed in more detail later in the chapter.

Local newspapers frequently carry classified ads, as do many consumer and trade magazines. A few publications, such as Exchange & Mart, are almost entirely devoted to this type of advertising.

Classified ads are usually charged at a price per word. You may be allowed to give some words additional emphasis by putting them all in capitals, but that's about it. It is therefore important that the words themselves are very carefully chosen. Good classified advertising should:

1. Assume the reader already has an interest in buying your product or service (or why would he be reading the advertisements under that category?).
2. Tell the reader as much as possible about the product within the number of words available.
3. Show the benefits to the reader of buying your product.
4. Create some relevant feeling about the product.
5. Tell the reader how to respond to the advertisement.
6. Compete effectively with other advertisements in the category.

The above list is best explained by reference to an example, so here is a successful ad which appears regularly in the 'Cornish' section of a national holiday magazine.

Charming waterside cottage, fully equipped for a quiet, independent, self-catering holiday, full central heating, luxury bathroom, dinghy available. Bodmin (00000) 000000.

In a few words, this advertisement gives the reader a lot of information about the holiday cottage. Warm feelings are created through use of words with positive associations such as 'charming' and 'luxury'. The dinghy is an additional benefit which helps the advertisement compete effectively with others in the category. And prospective visitors are given a phone number to call - a more direct, personal way of making contact than an address to write to (not to mention using fewer words).

WILL CLASSIFIED ADS WORK FOR YOU?

Whether classified advertising will work for your business depends largely on the trade you are in. Where people in your type of business regularly use classified advertising, and specialist categories exist for it in magazines and newspapers, it is certainly well worth considering.

To give you an idea, the types of business which regularly use classified advertising include:

- Hotels.
- Holiday homes.
- Hobbies.
- Introduction agencies.
- Business opportunities.
- Gift items.
- Charities.
- Mail order publishers.
- Printers.
- Collectors' items.

- Second-hand cars.
- Boating.
- Removals.
- Caravans.
- Educational courses.
- Building trades.

The best media to advertise in are those which contain a good number of classified ads for businesses of your type. These are the publications people are likely to turn to when they need a plumber/car dealer/introduction agency/holiday cottage, etc. You will, of course, be competing with other advertisers for trade. The art, as we shall see, is to write your ad in such a way that it stands out from the others.

WRITING YOUR CLASSIFIED AD

All too many classified ads give the impression that they have been dashed off in two minutes on the back of an envelope. This is a waste of the potential of what can be an extremely powerful and effective advertising medium. Be prepared to work hard on your classified ad, producing a series of rough drafts before the final, polished version. Follow the seven-step procedure below.

1. List all the user-benefits you can think of for your product or service (e.g. added security, available in five colours, buy two - get one free, lower price, special introductory offer, greater comfort, etc.).
2. Identify any points about your product or service which are unique, as these may be powerful selling points. Underline your USPs and the other benefits you think readers will find particularly attractive.
3. List any 'feelings' words which may help readers feel good or reassured about the product (charming, new, friendly, reliable, traditional, British standard, etc.).
4. Decide how many words are needed to either (a) tell your story, or (b) fit into the available space.
5. Write your advertisement. Then check it contains all the information and 'feelings words' which you decided were important from your list.
6. Compare your advertisement with others which are likely to appear in the same column, to ensure you are offering some benefits and feelings which they do not.
7. Re-read your effort and ask yourself: 'If I was looking for a product like this and I was to read this advertisement, would I be likely to respond?'

Bear in mind that some publications automatically put the first few words of classified ads in block capitals (whether you ask them to or not). Choose these words with particular care and attention, therefore. There is little value in having your ad begin with the words 'ARE YOU LOOKING FOR...' On the other hand an ad beginning 'CUT YOUR MOTORING COSTS' takes advantage of this opportunity to catch the reader's eye.

Don't be in too much of a hurry to write your classified ad and send it off. Advertising people have a saying: 'Give it a week.' Even if you can only afford to give it a day, with a fresh eye it is amazing how often you will see improvements you could make.

SELLING OFF THE PAGE

Can you sell your product 'off the page' from a classified ad? The answer depends very much on the price. In my experience, £10 or so is about the most people will send off for something advertised in the classifieds, and £5 or less is preferable. If your product costs more than this, you are likely to achieve better results from a two-stage procedure. For example, you could conclude your ad, 'Phone now for a free information pack', and send your advertising brochure, price list, testimonials, samples, etc. to people who reply.

SEMI-DISPLAY CLASSIFIED ADVERTISING

As mentioned earlier, many publications offer the option of semi-display advertising in their classified columns. Semi-display classified ads are normally surrounded by a border on all sides, and may include design features such as different typefaces, graphics, a logo, and even a small illustration or a photograph.

Semi-display classified ads are more eye-catching than lineage, but against this they are of course more expensive. They are usually paid for by the column centimetre rather than the number of words. If you want your message to stand out from your competitors' without breaking the bank, however, a semi-display classified ad may offer a cost-effective solution.

Semi-display advertisements generally include a caption or heading at the top. Avoid simply restating the category heading here. For example, if you are advertising in the holidays section, do not put 'Holiday Cottage', but 'Lake District', 'Devon' or whatever. People reading these ads already know that you are offering holiday accommodation. The first information they require is where it is. Similarly, if the column is headed cars, put the name of the car as your main heading ('Ford Escort 1.6 Ghia'), not 'Bargain', 'One Careful Owner', etc.

Publications will often design your semi-display classified ad for you, but the results are usually no more than serviceable.

Once you have found a form of words which seems to work well, it is worth paying a graphic artist or designer to prepare artwork for the advertisement. You can then make copies of this and use it with any publication you decide to advertise in.

MONITORING YOUR ADVERTISING

To use your advertising budget effectively, you need to know where all your orders and enquiries are coming from. It is therefore essential to monitor your advertising meticulously.

The usual method of monitoring responses to advertisements is by including some sort of keying device in the address. At its most basic, this may take the form of a 'Department' reference. For example, with an advertisement in the Weekly News you might use the address: Starlight Introductions, Dept. WN, PO Box 252...

A more subtle method is to include some variations in the way the address is spelt (as long as the Post Office can still deliver it). For example, in one publication you might use the address 52 Collins Road, in another 52 Colin's Road. You can even use variations on your business name, perhaps printing it in full in one publication, in an abbreviated form in another. According to the spelling on the envelope, you should then be able to work out where each enquiry has come from.

If your advertisement gives only a phone number, you will need to remember to ask all callers where they got your number (of course, many will tell you this anyway). You could also use the method suggested above of using a different business name in each publication. If a caller then asks for the Staydry Building Company you will know that they saw your advertisement in Magazine A, while if they ask for SBC they saw it in Magazine B. Your only problem then will be deciding how to answer the phone!

TESTING, TESTING...

Large companies are constantly testing and refining their advertising in light of the response it brings. As a small businessman aiming to grow, you can afford to do no less. Fortunately, the relatively low cost of classified ads means that they are an ideal medium for experimentation. Try different forms of wording, perhaps emphasising one customer benefit in one ad, another in a second. Allow each ad a reasonable trial - say half a dozen insertions. This will help even out any week-by-week variations.

Experiment, also, with placing your advertisements under different headings. For example, your mail order business guide may sell better if it is advertised under Business Opportunities rather than Publications - or the opposite may apply. You won't know until you've tried both. If your budget will stand it, you could try repeating your ad under various headings. Use a separate keying device with each, so that you can see which position brings in most enquiries and orders. If you are not getting the results you hoped for from advertising under the heading where you would normally expect to find your ad, Personal and Miscellaneous are two good alternatives to try.

You could also try comparing the pulling power of lineage advertisements against semi-display (taking the differing costs into account, of course). Finally, an under-used device definitely worth considering is to use a classified ad to draw attention to display advertising elsewhere in the publication. For example, a conservatory company with a regular display advertisement in a local paper might try a classified ad under the 'Builders' heading, such as: 'Looking for a beautiful, low-cost conservatory? See Sunbright Conservatories' advertisement on page 8.' Advertising departments will often give substantial discounts to regular advertisers, and may even let you have a small classified ad free. It's worth asking, anyway!

> *'A good ad should be like a good sermon; it must not only comfort the afflicted, it must also afflict the comfortable.'*

Bernice Fitzgibbon - American businesswoman

Once you have written a successful classified ad, keep repeating it until it starts to lose its 'pull'. Whereas with a display advertisement the same people are likely to see it week after week, people only tend to look at classified ads if they need the product or service at that time. There is therefore much less risk of people getting bored with your ad. Ask the publication to run the advertisement on a 'TF' basis ('TF' means 'Till Forbid'). They will then continue to run the ad until you cancel. They will also change the keying device for you every month if you wish.

WHEN SHOULD YOU ADVERTISE?
There is no doubt that advertising is more effective at certain times of the year than at others. Much depends on what you are selling. For many mail order businesses, for example, the best months are, in descending order of importance, October, November, September, January, February and March. The first three months of the year are good because people tend to be at home more, and have more time for reading and planning ahead. September, October and November also benefit from this factor, with the additional advantage that people are buying gifts for the

festive season. December can also be a good month for sales of giftware, but in many other areas (e.g. business-to-business, introduction agencies, correspondence courses, self-help books) sales decline as people become preoccupied with planning for the Christmas and New Year holiday.

It is sensible to be aware of these seasonal variations, in order to take advantage of the best times of year to advertise your particular product or service. Equally, being aware of the seasonal cycle can help you to avoid becoming too depressed if your classified ad in August fails to pull in much response. It can be a good tactic to even out demand over the year by offering extra incentives such as free gifts, price cuts and so on during traditionally quiet periods.

EXAMPLES

To conclude this chapter, here are a number of examples of successful classified ads. Look out for similar examples relevant to your own line of business. Bear in mind that the best test of a successful advertisement is that it is repeated week after week.

SIMPLY CORSICA. The most beautiful island in the Mediterranean. We offer villas with pools, seaside cottages, stylish hotels, mountain auberges, island wandering programme and flower and painting holidays. ABTA and ATOL bonded. 0000 000 0000.

Travel the world free and make money as you go - as a freelance writer and photographer. Literally thousands of markets desperate to buy anything and everything you write about your travels. New manual reveals all the closely guarded secrets: how to research, write and sell everything you write; how and where to sell every photo you take; get your fares/travel expenses paid in advance; free travel; how to work your way on ocean-going yachts/liners; plus much more, including a free guide to writers' grants and how to get them. For a priority copy, send £8.95 to....

RUN YOUR OWN DATING AGENCY - without any of the headaches! You find the clients - Perfect Match provides the know-how and all of the service. Full training provided - excellent business opportunity. Full or part-time. Ring 0000 000000.

All office furniture. Lowest prices. Biggest stocks. Save money! New/used. Ring the Midlands biggest supplier NOW! Birmingham 0000 000 0000.

FRANCE. Superb mobile homes on campsites by beautiful beaches. Up to three children under 14 years travel free. Travel two weeks for the price of one - May, June, September. Ring for brochure now! Matthews Holidays Ltd (ABTA 4293X) Tel. 00000 000000.

YOGA CLASSES for physical and mental well-being. Improve flexibility, posture and relaxation. Beginners welcome. Only £3.50 per class at the Iyengar Yoga Institute of South London. Close to New Cross BR and tube. Tel. 0000 000 0000.

EXECUTIVE CVs prepared by former chief personnel officer. Laser-printed, choice of styles. Reasonable rates. For free info pack call 0000 000000.

Alone Again? There's no need to be! For a very different approach to personal introductions, contact your local Perfect Match organiser, Shirley Smith, on 0000 000000.

FREE TRIAL! Successful professional punter reveals his own personal system which enables him to maintain a 70% strike rate at average odds of 3-1. Send no money now. Try it FREE for two weeks before deciding to keep it, or simply return it after your trial and owe nothing. Write to....

HIT THE JACKPOT WITH MULTI-SCOOP! The low-cost, computer-aided pools syndicate where everyone's a winner! Free details from....

GAS CENTRAL HEATING. All types fitted and repaired by ex-British Gas engineers. Combination boilers a speciality. Friendly, professional service. Call 00000 000000 for a free quote.

WORD PROCESSING by professional secretary/English graduate. Laser printing/diskette, all audio formats. From £3.00 per 1,000 words. Telephone 00000 000000.

Award-winning farm offers mouth-watering food, indoor heated swimming pool, snooker. 7 miles Pembrokeshire coast. Tel. 00000 000000.

Explore the Hebrides on the yacht Corryvreckan. Exciting sailing, excellent food, bird watching, whale spotting and exploring beautiful anchorages. All in luxurious comfort and with expert knowledge. Spaces available September and October. Douglas and Mary Smith. Tel/Fax 00000 000000.

KEY POINTS

- Classified ads are the cheapest and simplest form of advertising. They are usually charged at a price per word.
- It is best to advertise in publications where many similar businesses advertise. This will attract readers who need whatever it is that you are offering.
- When writing a classified ad, assume that the reader already has some interest in the product or service in question.
- Pay particular attention to the first few words of your ad. These are what readers see first, and some publications automatically give them extra emphasis.
- Show the reader the benefits of buying your product. Aim to create some relevant feelings towards it.
- At the end, make clear to the reader what he should do next (usually write or phone for more information).
- Study other published advertisements in your chosen category, to check that your ad will compete effectively with them.
- Give yourself as much time as possible to write your ad. With a fresh eye, it is often possible to see improvements which could be made.
- About the maximum people will send in response to a classified ad is £10, and £5 is preferable. If your product costs more than this, it may be better to adopt a two-stage strategy and use the ad simply as a means of generating enquiries.
- Semi-display classified ads are another option. They can help your ad stand out from others around it (though this must obviously be set against the extra cost).
- Avoid simply repeating the category heading at the top of your semi-display ad. Consider what is the first piece of information people scanning the category will want, and (unless you have a very good reason) use that as your heading.
- Once you have a form of words which works well, consider paying a graphic artist or designer to prepare artwork for you. You can then make copies of this to use with any publication you decide to advertise in.
- Constantly monitor the effectiveness of your advertising. Use a keying device such as a 'Department' reference, or give your address or business name differently for each publication.
- Experiment with classified advertising. Try using different category headings, or comparing the effectiveness of lineage and semi-display.
- Once you have found what works best for your business, stick with it until it starts to lose its pull. Because of the constantly changing audience for classified advertising, there is much less risk of readers becoming bored with your ad.
- Remember that all advertising works better at some times of

the year than others. Be prepared to take full advantage of the best times for your business, and consider offering special incentives to generate extra business during quiet periods.

CHAPTER FOUR

DISPLAY ADVERTISEMENTS

Classified ads work well for some products and services, and fortunes have been made on the back of them. For many businesses, however, display advertising may be a more effective and appropriate medium. Although more expensive than classified ads, display ads have a range of advantages:

1. They are more eye-catching and hence more likely to be noticed.
2. You have more space available to put across your sales message.
3. You can easily incorporate visual elements such as photos, drawings, logos and different typefaces.
4. Display ads help to give the impression that your business is a serious and substantial concern.
5. Where you want to gain the attention of casual browsers as well as people actively looking for your particular product or service, display ads are the only realistic option.

If you are thinking of using display advertising, it is a good idea to spend some time researching how other businesses use this medium. As with classified ads, seek out advertisements which are repeated time after time with only minor variations, as they are obviously successful in achieving the advertisers' objectives.

Look at businesses in your trade and in others. Keep and study carefully any advertisements you think work well. While I do not advocate copying other people's advertisements, there is nothing to stop you 'borrowing' their best ideas.

Display ads are charged for by the amount of space they take up - e.g. per single column centimetre (scc), which is a space one column wide and one centimetre deep. Publications may also quote the cost per 1/8, 1/4, 1/2 or full page. There may be an extra charge if you want your advertisement in a particular position, e.g. on the front or back cover.

HOW DO YOU PREPARE A DISPLAY ADVERTISEMENT?

Various options are available to you when preparing display ads:

1. Most newspaper and magazine publishers will prepare artwork for you in-house. All you supply is the wording and perhaps a rough sketch showing how you want your advert to look. Most publications offer this as a free service to display advertisers, and for straightforward adverts without frills the results are usually acceptable.

2. It is also possible to prepare your own artwork for display advertising, perhaps using one of the excellent desktop publishing programs now on the market. Some publications will accept laser-printed artwork, but perhaps the best option (especially when using colour) is to submit your advert on floppy disk in the form of a print file. All the publisher then has to do is load the disk into his own publishing set-up and it should appear on the printed page exactly as it looked on your computer screen. Most modern DTP programs include a facility to print to file, but it is as well to check with the publication concerned that they can accept advertisements in this format (see figure 1).

3. You can engage a designer or graphic artist to produce the necessary artwork for you. They will obviously require a fee for this, but once the job has been done you can make copies for each publication in which you wish your advertisement to appear.

4. Finally, you can put the whole thing in the hands of an advertising agency. This is likely to produce the most professional looking results, though it will also cost the most.

Even if you choose to go through an agency, it is important to have some ideas on what you want your advertisement to achieve and how it should go about doing this, and to this we will now turn our attention.

'Most advertising is absolutely awful, easily forgotten, invisible garbage. That's why most advertising is ignored.'

George Lois - American art director

Figure 1. This hard-working display advertisement was created by the advertiser himself using the desktop publishing program Microsoft Publisher, and submitted to the magazine on floppy disk.

WRITING YOUR DISPLAY ADVERTISEMENT

Even if you intend to use only the smallest of display ads - perhaps one column wide by a few centimetres deep - there are many more elements at your disposal than with a classified ad. These include the heading, illustrations, body text and (if appropriate) order/enquiry form. We will look at each of these in turn.

Heading

The heading, along with any illustrations, is the first thing a reader is likely to notice in your advertisement. Five times as many people read the heading as read the rest of the ad. It is therefore important that it attracts the reader's attention and impels him to go on reading. The heading should highlight the main benefit which is being offered to potential purchasers. A good heading tells readers at a glance, 'What's in this for me?' The simplest - and often best - technique is to state your main benefit:

- How to beat the bookmaker.
- Lose weight - the natural way.
- Windows, doors and conservatories at 1991 prices!
- Personal loans with guaranteed acceptance.

A variation is to start with a question.

- What paint do professionals use?
- Do you want to retire in three years' time with an income for life?
- Where can you buy a new computer for less than half the showroom cost?
- Looking for a more exciting holiday this year?

Either way, the aim is to attract the attention of your target readers - those who have a potential interest in buying your product or service - and enticing them to read on. Often the advert's effectiveness can be increased with a sub-heading which gives the reader a reason to believe the message in the main heading. For example:

Beat the bookmaker - combining our racing expertise with the latest computer technology

LOOKING FOR A MORE EXCITING HOLIDAY THIS YEAR? – JPL HAS BEEN RUNNING ADVENTURE HOLIDAYS ACROSS THE WORLD FOR MORE THAN TWENTY YEARS.

Illustrations

A good illustration will do a similar job to the heading in capturing readers' attention. Various options are available, including photographs, drawings or cartoons. Much depends on the media your advertisements will be appearing in. Photos reproduce poorly in newspapers, so for such media a line drawing or cartoon may be best. In glossy magazines, on the other hand, photographs can be highly effective, and more convincing than drawings.

The golden rule with photos or drawings is that they should show the product in action. Thus, rather than show just a video camera, a more effective illustration might show a mother using the camera to make a video recording of her family. Photos should combine well with the heading and body text, and increase the overall interest of the ad. A caption can be used if necessary to explain the picture, but avoid stating the obvious.

Body text

The body text of your advertisement has to arouse the reader's interest in the product and persuade (or start to persuade) him to buy. It should follow logically from the promise made in the heading. For example, if the heading is LOSE WEIGHT - THE NATURAL WAY, the body text should make clear exactly how the product concerned will help the user to lose weight naturally. This may appear to be stating the obvious, but a surprisingly large number of advertisements fail to deliver on the promise made in the heading.

Continue in the body text to set out your product or service's benefits - the more the better. To avoid missing anything out, it can be a useful exercise before writing your advert to list all the selling points you can think of. In the case of a restaurant, for example, these might include:

- Friendly atmosphere.
- Vegetarian choices available.
- Fixed price menu or à la carte.
- All major credit cards accepted.
- Spacious and comfortable.
- 16th Century farmhouse setting.
- Cordon Bleu chef.
- Michelin award.
- Real ales on tap.
- Extensive wine cellar.
- Separate room for large groups or parties.
- English and Italian cuisine.
- Entertainment on Friday and Saturday evenings.

Look out especially for USPs (Unique Selling Propositions). As mentioned in Chapter Three, these are benefits which are unique to your business; they can therefore be powerful selling points. 'The only Belgian restaurant in Folkestone' would be a USP, as would 'Sutton's only restaurant serving emu steaks'. It is not essential to have a USP, and few businesses have more than two or three. If you do have one, however, it is worth trying to capitalise upon it in your advertising.

The style in which body text is written bears careful consideration. Below are some guidelines:

Make your copy (advertising text) crisp and concise

No-one has to read an advertisement, so they are not the place for experiments in 'purple prose'. In small ads, a lists of benefits each preceded by a bullet point may be sufficient. In longer advertisements you may need to write in sentences and paragraphs, but keep both short and snappy.

Write from a customer's point of view

Avoid the temptation to talk about yourself and your business - when it was founded, how large it is, how much profit it made last year, and so on. This information is of little interest to customers. The text of your advertisement should address the customer's needs, answering the question 'What's in this for me?' Use the word 'you' frequently, while avoiding as far as possible the words 'I', 'me', 'we' and 'us'.

Aim for a friendly, informal style

Advertising has been described as 'salesmanship in print' - and the conversational tone of a good salesman should not change just because the words are in writing rather than in speech. Short, punchy sentences usually work best. Even ungrammatical sentences (like this one).

Avoid words and phrases that have become stale with over-use

Examples include 'fantastic offer', 'unbelievable bargain', 'superb opportunity', 'outstanding'. People have seen these expressions used so many times that they (rightly) regard them with suspicion. Try to find something new and interesting to say about your product.

Be honest in all your advertising

That means avoiding making extravagant promises which you cannot keep. Most people will not believe you; and if by chance they do, you will find yourself in difficulties when your product or service fails to measure up to their expectations.

Be aware of the emotional associations of words

For example, a client of mine in a charity submitted a draft advertisement aimed at older people which began with the words, 'Are you becoming old and losing your mobility? Has arthritis robbed you of the ability to go out, and confined you to a wheelchair?' This clearly defined the target audience, but it is full of cold words: old, losing, robbed, confined. Even people who could have benefited from the charity's services might have found it offputting. My rewritten version began, 'Do you need a little extra help to enjoy the good things of life...' The cold words were replaced by warm ones: extra, help, good, enjoy, life, and so on.

Write in the present tense

Thus, rather than put, 'This device will cut your fuel bills by ten per cent a year', write, 'This device cuts your fuel bills by ten per cent a year'. This is more direct, and encourages the customer to start to imagine that he has the product in question already.

Avoid talking about the price

Instead talk about value or worth to the customer. The price of an automatic dishwasher may be £300, but its value consists in time saved over the sink and available for more enjoyable activities instead. This is really another way of saying that you should focus on the benefits of your product or service to the customer, rather than features (such as price).

Study published advertisements to see the style used by the professionals

Some of this is undoubtedly too clever for its own good, but nevertheless much can be learned by examining how they are written. You may also find ideas which you can adapt to your own advertising.

Be prepared to rewrite and polish your work many times, until it is as good as you can possibly make it

A successful advertisement will repay many times over the time and effort you put into writing it. Some other ingredients worth considering for the body of your display ad include:

Endorsements

Quotes from published reviews and/or satisfied users can be effective, as readers are more inclined to trust the word of an 'objective' outsider. Avoid making up endorsements: you are likely to be found out and may fall foul of the law. On the other hand, there is nothing to stop you soliciting favourable comments. Publishers, for example, often send out advance copies of new titles to reviewers in the hope of getting good quotes for the back cover.

Special offers

These can also be highly effective. If you have a good offer (e.g. two for the price of one) it may be worth using this as a heading. At the very least your offer should feature prominently in the body text.

Offers are frequently used to give the reader a reason to respond immediately (a free gift for our first 100 customers, 20 per cent discount this week only). This is especially important in newspaper advertising, which is invariably discarded within a day or two.

Coupons

Similarly, a coupon entitling the holder to a free gift or discount can work well. The reader has to cut the coupon out, and through this physical action your advertising message will be stamped more firmly in his mind. Restaurants, in particular, have been very successful in using coupons to increase trade during slack periods. Coupons are really a form of sales promotion (discussed in Chapter 9): they attract new customers, some of whom - you hope - will become regulars.

Humour

A note of humour can undoubtedly help to make an advertisement stand out from its competitors. Against this, everyone has a different sense of humour, and if readers don't share yours they may be simply be confused or irritated by it. Using a cartoon can be one way around this problem. Even if some readers still don't get the joke, a cartoon will at least make clear that the intention was humorous.

White space

It can be tempting to aim to fill every square centimetre of your display advertisement (after all, you have to pay for it). This may be a mistake, however. Densely-written advertisements can be visually offputting, and tend to blend in with the surrounding material. By contrast, if you leave a generous border around the text of your advertisement, the white space will make the ad stand out, even from a distance. Some large companies have taken this to extremes, buying a whole page of a newspaper then putting a tiny advertisement in the middle. While extravagantly expensive, there is no doubt that this technique can be visually arresting.

Order/enquiry form

At the end of the advertisement, it is important to make clear to readers what they should do next ('Ring 0800 9000 now for an instant quote', 'Return the coupon below for a free brochure'). If space permits, a separate order or enquiry form which readers can fill in and send off has been proved to increase response. A Freepost address also boosts replies, though not usually to the same extent.

Whatever the size of your advertisement, make sure that your order form always comes at the bottom or - if it is not that big - the bottom right-hand corner of the page. The worst place for an order form is across the spine between two pages. No-one will bother to cut into the spine of a magazine to take out an order form.

Make the form as large as possible. Tiny forms will result in illegible names and addresses, and put off many potential respondents altogether. To avoid wasting hours trying to decipher illegible handwriting, it is a good idea to include an instruction to write in block capitals.

ADVERTORIAL

This is an increasingly popular variation on display advertising, although some publications still refuse to accept them. As the name suggests, advertorials are advertisements which have been presented to look like editorial (i.e. articles). Legally, there must be a heading stating that the item is an 'advertisement' or 'advertisers' announcement' (see figure 2).

Opinions vary about the merits of advertorials. Those in favour argue that because advertorials look like articles, readers are more likely to

Would you like to be a writer?
by NICK DAWS

Freelance writing can be creative, fulfilling and a lot of fun, with excellent money to be made as well. What's more, anyone can become a writer. No special qualifications or experience are required.

The market for writers is huge. In Britain alone there are around 1,000 daily, Sunday and weekly papers, and more than 8,000 magazines. Many of the stories and articles that they publish are supplied by freelances. Then there are books, theatre, films, TV, radio...

With such demand, there's always room for new writers. But, as Mr. E. H. Metcalfe, principal of Britain's leading writing school The Writers Bureau, explains; 'If you want to enjoy the rewards of seeing your work in print, one thing you must have is proper training.'

The Writers Bureau runs a comprehensive correspondence course covering every aspect of fiction and non-fiction writing. The 140,000 word course is written by professional writers and has been acclaimed by experts.

Students receive one-to-one guidance from tutors, all working writers themselves. From the start they are shown how to produce saleable work. 'At the Bureau our philosophy is quite simple' says Mr. Metcalfe. 'We will do everything in our power to help students become published writers.'

The course comes on fifteen days free trial. In addition, the Bureau offers a remarkable money-back guarantee - if you haven't earned your tuition fees from published writing within one month of completing the course, your money will be refunded in full.

So, would you like to be a writer? Why not start now by returning the coupon below!

Why Not Be A Writer?

First-class home-study course gets you a flying start. Earn while you learn. Expert tutors, personal guidance, help to sell your writing and much more! It's ideal for beginners. Details free. No cost. No obligation. Send the coupon.

Name ....
(BLOCK CAPITALS PLEASE)

Address ....

....

.... Postcode...............

The Writers Bureau Freepost AC2893,
Manchester M1 1JB   Freephone 0800 262382

Figure 2. An advertorial written by the present author. This advertisement has been run in newspapers and magazines several hundred times, and at the time of writing is still being used.

believe the message they contain. They also say that in an advertorial there is more room to put across your sales message than in an equivalent-sized display advertisement. Others, however, argue that it is foolhardy to assume that readers are unable to tell the difference between an advertisement and an article; and that if readers feel that an attempt is being made to con them, they are likely to respond negatively to the advertisers' message.

I cannot offer a definitive answer to this debate, only comment that, with the right product or service, advertorials can undoubtedly be effective. The advertisement in figure 2, with various minor variations, has been run by the correspondence school concerned several hundred times over the past six years, and has consistently out-performed more conventional types of advertising. Obviously, a business in another field might not achieve the same results.

If you would like to try using advertorials, the first step will be to contact the advertising department of your chosen publication. If it is not obvious from a study of the latest issue, check whether they do in fact publish advertorials. Publications which regularly include this type of advertising will not normally expect you to write the advertorial yourself; a staff journalist, or possibly a freelance, will interview you and prepare a piece for your approval. The cost will be included within the fee you are quoted.

If at all possible, try to have one or more photos or illustrations published alongside the piece; this will draw in many more readers than text alone.

'The best ad is a good product.'

Alan H. Meyer - Writer

ADVERTISING FEATURES

Many people are confused by the distinction between advertorials and advertising features. An advertising feature is an article produced by a newspaper or magazine designed to attract readers' attention and stimulate their interest in certain subjects. Popular topics for advertising features include:

- Christmas Shopping.
- Easter.
- Mother's Day.
- Weddings.
- Cars.
- Holidays.
- Gardening and home improvements.

Potential advertisers are contacted by the publication's advertising department and asked if they would like to place an advert in the space surrounding the article. It is not, however, possible to purchase advertising in the article itself. Good results can be obtained by advertising in advertising features, but check carefully when they are due to be published. Many are planned well in advance - and there is little point in booking an advertisement for an Easter or Christmas advertising feature if your business will be shut for the week when the relevant issue comes out.

Figure 3. "It's Brill at the Drill". One of a series of display ads run in local papers by this enterprising pub. A good example of how imaginative advertising can help build a business's image.

HOW LARGE SHOULD YOUR DISPLAY AD BE?

In general, the larger your advertisement, the more enquiries and orders it will generate. This is not necessarily a direct, mathematical link, however. In 'Successful Marketing for the Small Business', Dave Patten writes:

'Research shows that ads do not pull in proportion to their size. A whole page does not produce twice the number of responses as half a page, but only about 70 per cent more and so on pro rata.'

One moral of this is that it may be more effective to have two half-page ads in different places in a magazine rather than one full page; or alternatively two half-page ads in different magazines, rather than a full page ad in a single one. On the other hand, there is no doubt that a large advertisement gives an impression of solidity and reliability which may be important for some types of business, as well as being more eye-catching. As with so much in the world of advertising, hard and fast rules are impossible to give. The advice must be to experiment, find out what works best for your business, then stick to it.

BOOKING YOUR DISPLAY AD

The best position for an advertisement is on the back or inside covers, but these can be expensive and are often booked months in advance. A good place to try is near the reader's reply service (if the magazine has one), as many readers will turn to this page. The cheapest option is ROP ('run of paper') which is anywhere the magazine can fit it in.

It's always worth trying to negotiate a discount with advertising sales departments, especially if you are a subscriber, a local firm, a regular advertiser, willing to pay in advance, or any other excuse you can think of. As well as discounts on the standard rates, various types of special deal may be available. You will have to ask for these as they won't be offered automatically.

'PI' ('Per Inquiry')

In this type of deal you agree to pay the publication a fixed fee for each inquiry your advertisement brings in - and in exchange the advertisement is printed free of charge. To protect their own interest, the publication may insist that all responses to the ad are addressed to them, perhaps using a Box Number. They will then forward replies to you, and invoice you accordingly. PI deals are never advertised, but a surprisingly large range of publications will accept them.

'Help-if-needed'

A help-if-needed deal means that the publication will rerun your advertisement free of charge if you do not meet your expenses from your first ad. Such arrangements are usually made with the salesman representing the magazine in question. Help-if-needed deals may not be available with larger magazines, but smaller ones are often willing to assist in this way.

Stand-by advertising

This form of advertising is accepted by many newspapers and some magazines. This means that you send your advert to the publication concerned, and they keep it until they have space they need to fill at the last minute (e.g. due to another advertiser cancelling). Such advertising can be very cheap - as little as 20 per cent (or less) of the normal, quoted price. Some mail order publishing firms use stand-by advertising to get advertisements in national newspapers which would otherwise be uneconomical for them.

As far as frequency is concerned, bear in mind the old advertising adage 'Repetition is Reputation'. As I have already noted elsewhere, if you intend to advertise you should be prepared to advertise regularly. Despite what I have said about the effectiveness of a large advertisement for some types of business, if your budget presents you with a choice between one large advert once a month or a smaller ad once a week, it is almost certainly the latter you should choose.

MONITORING YOUR ADVERTISING

As with classified ads, it is important to monitor the performance of your display advertisements - arguably even more so, considering the larger sums involved. As described in the previous chapter, you can use keying devices in your address such as 'department numbers' to reveal the source of an enquiry. Cut-out coupons can be particularly useful here.

Ensure that any such coupons appearing in your ads carry a unique reference, and when they are presented by a customer you will know which of your advertisements it was that attracted them.

KEY POINTS

* Although more expensive than classified ads, display ads do have a number of advantages. In particular, they are better at catching the eye of casual browsers.
* If you intend to use display advertising, spend some time researching how other businesses use the medium. Keep a folder of successful display ads, and see if there are any ideas you could adapt in your own advertising.
* When preparing display ads you have a range of options: you can allow the publication to design your advertisement for you; you can prepare the artwork yourself; you can engage a graphic artist or designer; or you can use the services of an advertising agency.
* When writing your ad, the first thing to consider is the heading. This must attract readers' attention and encourage them to read on.
* Two popular choices for headings are stating your main benefit or asking a question. You could also incorporate a sub-heading to increase the interest still further.
* A good illustration can do a similar job to the heading in capturing readers' attention. The options available include a

photograph, line drawing or cartoon.

- Photos and drawings should always show the product in action. Include human beings where possible as well as the product itself.
- Body text should follow logically from the promise made in the heading. It should set out as many as possible of the product's benefits and USPs (Unique Selling Propositions).
- The text of the advertisement should be crisp and concise, and written from the reader's point of view. Keep the style friendly and informal.
- Be honest in all your claims, avoiding advertisers' clichés such as 'exceptional bargain'.
- Be aware of the emotional associations of words. Use 'warm' words when you want to create positive feelings in readers, not 'cold' ones.
- Write body text in the present tense. This will encourage readers to start imagining that they have the product already.
- Avoid talking about the cost or the price - instead talk about the value or worth to the customer.
- Be prepared to polish and rewrite your ad many times until you believe it is as good as you can possibly make it.
- Consider using devices such as endorsements, coupons and special offers to increase the response to your display ads.
- Humour can help make an advertisement stand out, but there is a risk it will be misinterpreted. Cartoons can provide a very effective solution.
- Avoid the temptation to fill every square centimetre of your display ad. Having some white space increases readability, and can make your ad more eye-catching.
- At the end of the advertisement, make it clear what you want your reader to do next. A form to fill in and return is a good idea, but make it as large as possible to avoid problems with illegible handwriting.
- Advertorials can be very effective for some kinds of business. An advertorial is written to look, at first glance anyway, just like an ordinary article.
- An advertising feature based around a theme such as Easter or Holidays can provide a good opportunity for advertisers, but be sure to check when it will actually appear.
- As far as size is concerned, two half page advertisements may be more effective than one whole page.
- When booking your ad, it is always worth trying to negotiate a discount. You could also ask for a 'PI' or 'Help-if-needed' deal, and investigate the possibility of stand-by advertising.
- Monitor all your advertising carefully, using keying devices, coupons, and so on.

CHAPTER FIVE

SALES LETTERS

Although print advertising uses up the major part of many businesses' advertising budgets, sales letters fulfil an important, and complementary, role. Their wide range of uses include:

- Writing to existing customers bringing new offers to their attention.
- Writing to former customers encouraging them to return.
- Writing to potential customers (whose names may have been obtained from directories or list brokers) offering your services.
- Writing to people who have contacted you as a result of press coverage or an advertisement.

In addition, if you sell your product via retailers or wholesalers, letters can be useful for keeping in touch and letting them know about new models, sales promotions, point-of-sale material and so on.

A sales letter may or may not ask for an order straight off - the aim may simply be to bring the customer into your shop, or get him to send for a full information pack. The letter may be sent on its own, or it may form part of a package including a leaflet, price list, samples, etc. Here we are starting to stray into the area of direct response, discussed in detail in the next chapter. In this chapter we will look at the sales letter itself, focusing on three main areas: content, style and appearance.

'Advertising is what you do when you can't go to see somebody. That's all it is.'

Fairfax Cone - American advertising executive

CONTENT

A good sales letter meets the AIDA specification. It...

1. Attracts ATTENTION
2. Arouses INTEREST
3. Stimulates DESIRE to purchase
4. Prompts the reader to take some ACTION

Attract attention

A sales letter does not need to grab attention as vociferously as an advertisement. Whereas an advert may be competing with dozens of others on the same page for readers' attention, when someone opens your letter you have, however briefly, his undivided attention.

Nevertheless, it is the easiest thing in the world for a reader to throw your letter away unread. Many sales letters therefore begin by gaining the reader's attention with an arresting heading. In a sales letter, the usual place for this is after (or even above) the salutation ('Dear Sir/Madam...'). Here are a few examples of attention-grabbing headings from sales letters I have received recently. Notice, incidentally, how they all incorporate the word 'you'.

- Are YOU paying too much for your phone bills? (Letter from telephone company).
- Up to £3,000 to help you when you need it most. (Financial services company).
- Throw this away and you are throwing away a potential £1,000 a week! (Business opportunity offer).
- Make this summer one you will always remember. (Conservatory company).

Not all sales letters require headings. One example would be if you are writing with details of a special offer to a regular customer whom you are confident will be interested in what you have to say. In this case, you may judge that there is no need to 'shout' to get his attention. When writing to new prospects, however, giving your sales letter a heading is often a good idea.

Arouse interest

Having assured yourself of the prospect's attention, the next step is to gain his interest. To achieve this, your letter must answer the question, "What's in this for me?" People buy products or services because of the benefits they think they will obtain from owning or using them. Examples of possible benefits include:

- Increase income.
- Save money.
- Be healthier.
- Live longer.
- Be more attractive.
- Improve career prospects.
- Raise self-esteem.
- Outdo others ('snob value').
- Protect one's home and possessions.

The opening paragraph of your letter should show clearly the main benefit you are offering. You could begin with a quotation, a question, a statement or an instruction. You might even begin by suggesting the complete opposite of what you want your prospect to do. Here are some examples of opening paragraphs, each referring to one particular main benefit.

Increase income

How would you like to run your own business? A business you can start for less than a few hundred pounds. A business with low overheads. A business which is totally home-based. And a business which can be operated part- or full-time.

Save money

If you live in a hard water area, you could be literally pouring money down the drain...(letter advertising water softeners).

Be healthier

"Research shows that if you lower your blood cholesterol by 1 mmol/litre, you will halve your risk of a heart attack," says Dr Elizabeth Forbes. (letter advertising low cholesterol diet book).

Improve career prospects

Don't bother to read this letter - if you have no interest in obtaining a better job. (letter from correspondence college).

Raise self-esteem

Are you a normally confident person who becomes tongue-tied and awkward when asked to make a speech, propose a vote of thanks, or take the chair at a meeting? Then you are one of the people for whom this book has been specially written.

Outdo others
As someone who appreciates the good things of life, we felt you should be among the first to receive news of our finest yet range of exotic foods and wines.

Protect home and possessions
Every ten seconds somewhere in the UK, another private house is burgled. (letter from home security company).

Stimulate desire to buy
Having aroused your prospect's interest, you must now start to stimulate the desire to buy. To do this, you must show how your product will be of benefit to the prospect. If he does not know anything about the product, you must describe it and show clearly what it will do.

It is essential to describe your product from the prospect's point of view. Vague comments such as 'great value', 'superb opportunity' and 'best on the market' are unlikely to be effective. Instead, highlight specific features of your product which make it stand out from its competitors. If you are selling a correspondence course, for example, your letter might stress the quality of the course material, the professional qualifications of the tutors, the unconditional money-back guarantee, and so on. The example below stresses these points, and shows the approach to adopt.

> *Our comprehensive 120,000 word course is divided into 32 study modules, each of which was written by an acknowledged expert in the field. Our tutors are all working professionals, and have been specially selected for their enthusiasm and ability to pass on their expertise to their students. We are confident you will enjoy studying with us, and offer this unique guarantee - if you have not earned back your entire course fee within a month of completing the course, your money will be refunded in full...*

An alternative approach when describing the features of a product is to include a list of points, each preceded by a dash, an asterisk or a bullet point (this is similar to the approach used in many display ads). The sales letter from Way Ahead later in this chapter uses this style.

Description can be particularly effective if it is accompanied by comparison. I do not, in general, advocate comparing another company's products unfavourably with your own. (This is known as 'knocking copy', and can backfire badly if your competitors decide to retaliate in kind). However, if you can in some way compare your product with another which is well known and respected in a different field, some of the other product's reputation can rub off on yours. For example, if you sell fax machines, you might describe your top-line model as 'the Rolls Royce of the fax world'. This creates an impression of smoothness and reliability which is very much the type of image you might wish to convey.

A similar approach is to draw comparisons with well-known people. For example, a letter beginning 'Fancy yourself as another Richard Branson...' might strike a chord with many budding entrepreneurs. Whatever claims you make about your product, it is important to provide evidence to substantiate them. This can take various forms:

* Scientific evidence.
* Government statistics.
* Facts and figures.
* Quotes from satisfied customers.
* Endorsements from experts.
* Quotes from published reviews.
* Guarantees.
* Samples of the product.

Your aim is to 'prove' to readers that everything you claim in your letter is true, and that they have nothing to risk by responding to your offer. Avoid, however, the temptation to embroider evidence, or even make things up. Making false or exaggerated claims is against the law - and anyway, your good reputation, on which your business ultimately depends, requires that you should always be honest in your advertising.

Prompt the reader to take action

At the end of the letter, you must make clear what action you want the reader to take next: place an order, visit your showroom, send for a free information pack, etc. Make it as easy as possible for him to respond, e.g. by filling in an enquiry or order form at the end of the letter. Even better is a separate, pre-printed, post-paid reply card, where all the prospect has to do is write down his name and address and put the card in a postbox.

You should also give the prospect a good reason WHY he should respond. For example:

'If you will send in the enclosed enquiry card (ACTION), we will send you a free information pack showing how the Bettercall fax/phone/modem can revolutionise your business communications (REASON).'

It is a good idea to give your reader a reason to act immediately. This may be a special discount for a limited period, or a free gift if they reply within 14 days. The aim is to get your prospect to respond NOW. If they decide to leave it for another day, there is a good chance that your offer will be forgotten about.

SAMPLE SALES LETTER

The letter below was sent by a computer software company to past customers (who had bought its small business or creative writing training software) to inform them of a new product launch, and hopefully obtain orders. It illustrates many of the principles described so far in this chapter.

Dear Way Ahead Customer

Become a marketing expert with Business Acumen Marketing

Way Ahead has great news for you. Our brand new tutorial, Business Acumen Marketing, will be released later this month and we are offering it at a special discount for all existing Way Ahead customers. If you are starting a new business or building up an existing one, or if you are a writer wishing to break into the world of public relations or marketing, you will find this program invaluable.

Business Acumen Marketing, which features a beautifully graphical, point-and-click interface, runs in Microsoft Windows on the IBM or compatible PC. Main features include:

- Marketing material, like press releases, marketing plans, sales letters and advertisements, which makes it simple for you to produce your own material.
- Glossaries which explain all the jargon, buzz-words and technical terms associated with marketing.
- Case studies, featuring businesses large and small, which show you by example how to achieve results.
- Learning text - all of which can be copied to your word processor or desktop publishing package - presented in scrollable windows.
- Checklists to assess your progress in every discipline involved in marketing.
- Tests which ensure that you have learned the lessons in each of the topics.
- A full tutorial which shows you in detail how to use Business Acumen Marketing to best advantage.

Business Acumen Marketing *is a complete marketing kit on your PC. Business users will find their marketing skills improve quickly,* *bringing better performance and bigger profits. Writers who use the tutorial to learn about marketing and then begin writing material for some of the many firms currently seeking help in this vital area will find their incomes increase substantially. Way Ahead has produced a unique guide -* **HOW TO MAKE GOOD MONEY WRITING FOR BUSINESSES AND OTHER ORGANISATIONS** *- which provides invaluable help in obtaining your first commissions in this exciting area of writing. Simply tick the option on the form at the bottom of the enclosed Business Acumen information sheet. Return your order within the next 21 days and you will receive the guide* **ABSOLUTELY FREE.**

Research shows that, of the high number of businesses that fail, a high proportion do not develop the right **marketing strategy**. Many do not know precisely who their products and services are aimed at, and have little or no experience of producing effective **marketing material**.

As a new or experienced writer, you can make a well-paid full- or part-time career out of writing advertisements, letters, press releases and other material vital to the sales success of all types of firm. However, if you know little or nothing about marketing, you will miss out on these genuine opportunities.

If you are **starting a business**, or have already started up and find you need more marketing knowledge and skills, the small investment in Business Acumen Marketing will pay for itself hundreds, probably thousands, of times over. Should you be one of the many writers who have their own businesses - which could be self-publishing or perhaps something unrelated to your writing work - Business Acumen Marketing will be doubly helpful.

So why not award yourself a BA (Business Acumen) Marketing today?

The normal price of the tutorial is £69.99 plus £2 p & p. However, because you are a valued Way Ahead customer, you can purchase **Business Acumen Marketing for JUST £49.99** plus £2 p & p. If you would like a preview before you buy, a demonstration disk is available for just £5 - and that £5 is redeemable against the price of the full Business Acumen Marketing package.

We are pleased to be able to offer you this truly exceptional tutorial at such an attractive price, and are certain that you will find it a great boon in your business or writing career, or both. For further information and an order form, see the enclosed sheet 10 Easy steps to a BA Marketing.

Yours sincerely...

This example of an actual sales letter follows many of the recommendations in this chapter. It begins with a headline: **'Become a Marketing Expert with Business Acumen Marketing'.** This striking claim attracts attention, and also sets out the main benefit the sender is offering.

As mentioned, the letter was sent to previous customers who fell into two distinct categories: small business owners and aspiring writers. Arguably it might have been better to send a different letter to each group, but for various practical reasons the seller decided to mail them all together. The first paragraph therefore identifies the letter's two target audiences with the line, 'If you are starting a new business or building up an existing one [BUSINESSES], or if you are a writer wishing to break into the world of public relations or marketing [WRITERS], you will find this program invaluable.'

The letter goes on to describe specific features of the product, using a list with bullet points. Notice how, as recommended, features are presented from the user's, rather than the seller's, point of view (e.g. 'Marketing material...which makes it simple for you to produce your own material', 'Case studies, featuring businesses large and small, which show you by example how to achieve results'). Notice, also, how almost every item in the list uses the word, 'you' and/or 'your'.

The letter then gives substantiating evidence about the importance of marketing for businesses, and of the money-making potential for writers entering this field. Further reassurance is provided by the discount price and the opportunity of purchasing a £5 demonstration disk before investing in the complete tutorial. Finally, the letter tells readers what action they should take next - 'For further information and an order form, see the enclosed sheet 10 Easy steps to a BA Marketing.' The latter was a separate order form which also included illustrations of the product in action.

The above letter was successful in terms of attracting enquiries and orders, but it is possible to see ways in which it could have been improved. As already suggested, the letter might have been more effective if two separate versions had been prepared for business customers and 'writing' customers, emphasising the specific benefits to each. And while the writer made a good job of listing features from a user's point of view, the letter might have been even more effective with stronger substantiating evidence. Specific facts and figures about the importance of marketing would have made it appear more authoritative, while quotes from reviews and satisfied users would have provided additional reassurance.

STYLE

Almost as important as the content of your sales letter is the style in which it is written. I have already mentioned the importance of writing your letter from the point of view of the recipient, answering the implied question 'What's in this for me?' The style should be warm and friendly, almost conversational in tone. The letter should flow well, so that reading it is a smooth, effortless process. The ten tips below will help you to achieve all this. They apply to all business correspondence, not only sales letters.

Use short words

Most people have an average vocabulary of around 5,000 words, less than 3,000 of which they use regularly. If your letter uses long, unusual words such as 'provenance' or 'contemporary', a proportion of readers will not understand what you mean. Rather than make the effort of looking in a dictionary, they are much more likely to give up.

For this reason, use short, simple, familiar words wherever possible. So instead of 'endeavour' write 'try'; rather than 'accede', put 'agree'; and instead of 'remittance', write 'payment' or 'fee'. As well as avoiding problems of comprehension, our eyes take in short words faster, making reading a quicker, less laborious process, especially for those with limited reading skills.

Use short sentences

Short sentences are easier to understand than long ones. They give a letter pace and improve its readability. Many long sentences are simply a set of short sentences which have been strung together. For example:

> *Further to your letter of the 7th April and fax message of the 19th April, I have to inform you that the items you requested were not in stock when we first received your order, but you will no doubt be pleased to hear that we have just taken delivery of a fresh consignment from the manufacturers, and your order is being despatched to you later today, with apologies for any inconvenience caused by the delay.*

This long-winded example is fairly typical of much modern business correspondence. See how much more effective it is when rewritten using short, reader-friendly words and sentences.

> *Thank you for your letter dated 7 April and fax of the 19th. I am sorry the items you asked for were out of stock when your letter arrived. We received new supplies today, and I am glad to say your order will be sent this afternoon. I am very sorry for any problems caused by the wait.*

One way of reducing sentence length is to cut out long-winded, hackneyed phrases. Examples include 'general consensus of opinion' (which can be replaced by the one word 'consensus'), and 'at this moment in time' (for which put 'now'). Below is a list of more such phrases, together with shorter alternatives.

We acknowledge receipt of	Thank you for
In view of the fact that	Since, as or because
In conjunction with	With
For the purpose of	To
In accordance with	In line with
It is our understanding that	We understand
Under separate cover	Separately
The undersigned	I or me
We are of the opinion that	We believe or we think
With reference to	About, concerning
With regard to	About, concerning
Advise us as to	Let us know
At which time	When
Are not in a position to	Cannot
In lieu of	In place of
Notwithstanding	Even if, despite, still, but
In the event of	If
In order to	To
If this is not the case	If not
If this is the case	If
For the duration of	During
Cognisant of	Aware of, know about
As a consequence of	Because

As a general guideline, aim for an average sentence length of 15 - 20 words. This does not prevent you writing some sentences which are longer or shorter than this (indeed, varying sentence lengths can help create a natural, conversational rhythm). However, if you can keep to this average, your letters should automatically become much more readable.

Use short paragraphs
Few things make a letter appear more off-putting than huge blocks of type. Such paragraphs look like hard work, and human nature being what it is many people will decline the challenge. For this reason alone, it is a good idea to break your letters into short paragraphs containing no more than four or, at most, five sentences.

There is, however, another reason for using plenty of short paragraphs, and this is that it will make your letter easier to understand. A paragraph is a unit of meaning, and should concern just one main topic. When a reader comes to a paragraph break, he is conditioned to expect some fresh point to be made or a change in the subject under discussion. If such a change comes in mid-paragraph, the reader will not be mentally prepared and may experience a jolt. Consider the example letter from an insurance broker below:

As you will no doubt know, motor insurance is a highly competitive sphere, but with our modern computerised system we can check the prices from hundreds of different insurance companies in seconds and find the best deal for YOU! Whether you are a new or old driver, have an unblemished record or a few 'blips', drive a Rolls Royce or a Reliant Robin, we are confident we can get you a better deal. House insurance is another area where we may be able to help. Many people remain, year after year, with the company which provided the insurance when their mortgage was taken out. If this applies to you, the odds are high that you are not getting the best possible value for money...

Did you notice a slight jolt when the writer suddenly switched from talking about motor insurance to house insurance? A paragraph break at that point would have signalled the change of subject, and avoided distracting the reader's attention.

Avoid slang, jargon and (most) abbreviations

Almost every trade and profession develops a jargon of its own. Computer people talk blithely about RAM, ROM, 'booting up' and bytes, while for those in PR it is photo calls, press releases, media briefings and press packs. When addressing people with a similar background to yourself, jargon can provide a quick and convenient way of sharing information and avoiding long, unnecessary explanations. However, misunderstandings can arise when communicating with people who do not share your specialist knowledge. When writing a sales letter, therefore, it is important to put yourself in readers' shoes and ask whether you have used any words or expressions which they might not understand.

Jargon terms often become second nature, and it is easy to forget that people outside your own sphere may not understand them. The same can apply to acronyms (words which are made up from the initial letters of a phrase, e.g. ICOM - Industrial Common Ownership Movement) and abbreviations.

If you work in agriculture, for example, the words CAP and AWB may be second nature to you, but someone working in a different sphere might be unaware that they stand for Common Agricultural Policy and Agricultural Wages Board respectively. If there is any doubt in your mind as to whether the recipient of your letter will understand any particular abbreviation, it is best to write it out in full.

Finally, beware of terms borrowed from other languages. People sometimes use these to make their letters look more authoritative or learned, but there is more likelihood that you will simply confuse and irritate a proportion of your readers. A selection of such words and terms, with suggested alternatives in plain English, is given below.

Apropos	About, concerning or with reference to
Ad hoc	For this purpose or occasion
Ceteris paribus	Other things being equal
Circa	About
De minimis	Trivialities, small amounts
Ex officio	By virtue of his/her job
Inter alia/alios	Among other things/people
Ipso facto	By that fact itself
Modus operandi	Way of working
Mutatis mutandis	With the necessary changes
Per se	As such, by itself
Pro forma	A form
Proximo	Of next month
Sine die	Indefinitely
Ultimo	Of last month
Via-a-vis	As regards, concerning, about
Viz (videlicet)	Namely

Write as you would speak
For some reason, many business people feel obliged to write in a stilted, formal style quite different from their normal, everyday speech. Whatever they might intend, the result can be highly off-putting for readers. Consider the two examples below:

Welcome to your new home! Right now, we're sure that buying new windows and doors is the last thing on your mind. But (dare we say it?) with winter only a few months away, now is the time any work should really be done. As we well know (having moved to larger premises ourselves only last year), moving is an expensive process. So to help, we've put together a special package which will help to spread the cost of any work you might want doing...

RE: 16 Park Crescent. We note that you have recently taken occupation of the aforementioned-mentioned property. As a local business of thirty years' standing, we are therefore taking this opportunity to draw to your attention the comprehensive range of products and services provided by our company. We can supply replacement window frames, porches and conservatories, all at highly competitive prices...

Which company would you rather do business with? In all probability, it is the one which sent the first letter. The tone comes across as helpful, friendly and informal, while that of second is cool and detached.

So how do you ensure that your letters have this conversational quality? Following the advice given earlier about avoiding long words, sentences and paragraphs will help, as will cutting out abbreviations and jargon. Varying the length of sentences and paragraphs will give a more natural conversational tone and help prevent monotony.

In addition, feel free to start some of your sentences with 'And' or 'But'. We all do it in day-to-day speech and, despite what your English teacher may have told you, there is nothing grammatically wrong with this. (You will, incidentally, be in good company, as Shakespeare, the Bible and Dickens all begin some sentences this way.)

Finally - as mentioned at the start of the chapter - aim to write from the reader's point of view. Give him the facts, avoiding exaggerated claims, superlatives ('the greatest ever!'), advertisers' clichés ('highly competitive prices') and 'hype'. In all selling, your aim is to build a relationship of trust with the customer. By adopting a style which is both friendly and factual, you will help reassure the reader that he will receive good, honest service from you and your company.

Use active rather than passive voice
The following is an example of a sentence written in the active voice:

William drove the car.

And here is the same sentence in the passive voice:

The car was driven by William.

Placing the subject of the sentence - the person or thing performing the action - in front of the verb (the 'doing' word) will usually ensure that the sentence is in the active voice. The active voice is more concise, more personal and easier to understand. The passive voice, in contrast, tends to be associated with the dead hand of bureaucracy:

PASSIVE VOICE	ACTIVE VOICE
It has been decided that...	We have decided...
A decision has been made that...	We have decided...
Your enquiry is being dealt with by...	We are dealing with your enquiry.

Sales letters, which aim for a friendly, conversational tone, should use active rather than passive voice most of the time. Just occasionally, however, the passive voice can be useful, e.g. when you want to focus the reader's attention on the object of the sentence (the thing which is acted on) rather than the subject. For example:

Our new model Samphire was voted Car of the Year by motoring journalists.

Use connecting words and phrases

Connecting words and phrases help readers by showing how sentences and paragraphs are connected with one another. Examples used in speech include 'what's more', 'so', 'in any case', 'apart from that', 'anyway' and 'otherwise'. More formal connectives used mainly in writing include 'however', 'in addition', 'furthermore', 'in spite of this', and many others. Letters making good use of connectives flow smoothly and logically, carrying the reader effortlessly along with them. Those with poor use of connectives, in contrast, seem to stutter from one point to another, causing readers great difficulty in following the thread of what is being said.

Connectives are often used at the start of a sentence or paragraph to show how the information which follows is related to what came before. For example, if a paragraph begins with 'Furthermore' the reader is alerted to the fact that more information supporting the writer's argument is about to be given. But if the new paragraph begins 'On the other hand', he immediately knows that a change of direction is coming. For this reason, connectives are sometimes known as signposting phrases. Readers do not normally pay much attention to connectives, but their presence helps them follow your argument and understand the case you are presenting. Although connectives are unobtrusive, changing one can totally alter the tone and meaning of your writing. Consider the examples below:

1. Our latest computer-based tutorial has many brand new features. Indeed, it includes ten interactive quizzes.
2. Our latest computer-based tutorial has many brand new features. However, it includes ten interactive quizzes.

The first of these examples suggests that the interactive quizzes are new, while the second suggests the complete opposite. These two examples demonstrate the power and importance of connectives in ensuring that your writing flows smoothly and logically.

Use vertical lists

The value of lists in sales letters has already been mentioned, and there is no doubt that they can be a great asset in all areas of business writing. Lists help break up solid blocks of text on the page, and make complex information far easier to read and assimilate. In the sales letter from Way Ahead reproduced earlier, a list was used to set out the main features of the tutorial. If instead the features had been set out in a conventional paragraph, few readers would have bothered to wade through the resulting raft of text.

The items in a list can be introduced with a bullet point, an asterisk or a dash followed by a space. Each point should, however, follow logically from the lead-in phrase or sentence.

The example below shows the kind of mistake which is frequently made.

The aims of our company are:

- to provide a first rate service to all our customers
- generating sufficient profit to finance future investment and research
- while remaining at the forefront of technological innovation
- staff training and development is a top priority
- constantly expanding our range of products and services

This reads awkwardly, as only the first of these five points follows logically (and grammatically) from the lead-in phrase. To read well, each of these points needs to begin with the word 'to'. The list could then be rewritten as follows:

The aims of our company are:

- to provide a first rate service to all our customers
- to generate sufficient profit to finance future investment and research
- to remain at the forefront of technological innovation
- to train and develop staff so that they may achieve their full potential
- to constantly expand our range of products and services

There is no generally agreed correct way of punctuating a list. In general, I advise introducing a list with a colon as above (and NOT a colon followed by a dash). If the list consists of a number of short phrases, each one should begin with a lower case (small) letter. You can then dispense with punctuation at the end of each item; or, if you prefer, end every one with a semi-colon, apart from the last item which you end with a full stop. Using this latter method, the above example then becomes:

The aims of our company are:

- to provide a first rate service to all our customers;
- to generate sufficient profit to finance future investment and research;
- to remain at the forefront of technological innovation;
- to train and develop staff so that they may achieve their full potential;
- to constantly expand our range of products and services.

Finally, if your list consists of complete grammatical sentences, it may be more appropriate to start each item with a capital letter, and end each with a full stop.

The Chairman made the following main points:

- The gross turnover of the company had increased by 15 per cent during the last financial year.
- Profits had increased by 20 per cent, due mainly to greater efficiencies in use of plant and improved terms obtained from suppliers.
- To counter a slight downturn in sales, an aggressive marketing campaign was planned to begin in the spring.

Use simple punctuation

In a way this follows from my earlier point about keeping sentences short. If you use mainly short sentences, then most of the time simple punctuation is all you will need.

The most valuable punctuation marks of all are full stops. They should be used freely. Commas can be helpful where they make your meaning easier to understand, but if you use mainly short sentences they should not be needed too often. The only other punctuation mark you are likely to require on a regular basis is the question mark - which, of course, must be placed at the end of any direct question.

- Is this the opportunity you are looking for?

- May we help you with your decorating requirements?
- How many boxes do you wish to order?

Other punctuation marks can be useful from time to time. The last sentence of the paragraph above included a dash. This can be a handy device if you wish to show that a sentence is taking off in a new and perhaps surprising direction ('The Dustmaster cleaner costs just £25.99 - less than half the price of other leading models').

As already mentioned, a colon (:) should be used to introduce a list (without an accompanying dash). Semi-colons (;) are unlikely to be needed in sales letters - not least because many people are unsure how to read them. If, nevertheless, you wish to include one, make sure you are using it correctly. A semi-colon should normally be placed between two independent clauses - which for practical purposes means two separate sentences. A good test is that it should be possible to replace the semi-colon with a full stop (but then, why not use a full stop in the first place?).

Finally, don't neglect apostrophes. They are required in contractions such as can't and won't, where they show that one or more letters has been omitted. They are also needed in expressions showing possession or association (the customer's choice, five years' service). Apostrophes are NOT required in present tense verbs (runs, walks, sells) or in plurals (taxis, videos, bananas, bargains). More and more people seem unable to get apostrophes right; but if you are writing to professional people in particular this can create a poor first impression.

In a book of this nature there is not the space to go into great detail about punctuation. If this is a problem area for you, two useful books to study are 'Mind the Stop' by G.V. Carey (Penguin) and 'The Cassell Guide to Written English' by James Aitchison.

Polish, polish, polish

Lastly, remember that even professional writers don't expect to get it all right first time. Be prepared to go back over your letter, checking for spelling and punctuation, and revising for the other qualities described in this chapter. The more time you can devote to your sales letter, the better the finished item is likely to be.

APPEARANCE

Along with an effective content and style, appearance is the third ingredient of successful sales letters. Let's start with the first thing a prospect sees when he opens the envelope...

Your letterhead

Letterheads are, in my view, an area where far too many business people are willing to compromise. Many use simply their business name, perhaps with the initial letters picked out in bold type to give some semblance of design. This is a waste of a good opportunity to advertise. To ensure your letterhead stands out, follow the guidelines below:

1. If at all possible, include an illustration showing what you do. A plumber could use a tap, a designer a drawing board, a decorator a paint-brush, etc.
2. If this is not possible, at least spell out in words what you do ('F.J. Sampson - Sanitary Engineers')
3. Alternatively, use an illustration of your business premises. This is obviously most appropriate if your offices are somewhere attractive and/or prestigious.
4. Make sure all the information customers need is clearly and conveniently set out. This applies especially to phone and fax numbers.
5. Consider using a short phrase or slogan which sums up what you do or your main customer benefit, e.g. The finest wines from around the world (wine merchant) - Putting words to work (advertising copywriter) - Keeping the wheels of industry turning (lubricants company).

There is little point in using heavyweight paper with silver- or gold-embossed lettering, unless perhaps you are trying to appeal to a very up-market clientele. Recipients will only conclude that you have money to burn (and hence are charging too much); or alternatively that you are desperate to project a successful image, and either crooked or about to go under.

Salutation

How you greet your prospect is worthy of consideration. If at all possible, personalise the letter to each recipient (this is discussed in more detail in the next chapter). If you don't know whom exactly you are addressing, try to avoid 'Dear Sir or Madam' as this has a cold, impersonal ring. Better alternatives include 'Dear Colleague', 'Dear Sports Lover', 'Dear Parent', 'Dear Friend', 'Dear Business Opportunity Seeker', and so on.

Sub-headings

Long letters often benefit from being broken up by sub-headings. Magazines and newspapers do this, and it can be instructive to study their technique. The best such examples pique the reader's curiosity, and defy him NOT to want to read the article itself. Use this technique in your own letters, choosing sub-headings which will intrigue the casual browser and 'hook' him into reading the letter itself.

Sub-headings can also help make long letters more readable, by providing a visual break and a point of reference for readers to refer to. On the other hand, they can also interrupt the smooth flow of a letter, and in some cases (for example when you are presenting a complete story, or arguing a single, complex case) it may be better to dispense with them.

Giving extra emphasis

Important phrases and sentences in your letter can be given extra emphasis by a variety of methods. These include single, double and triple underlines, capitals, italics, emboldening, different/larger typefaces and colour. A good word processor is obviously a great asset here, and allows you to experiment with different effects until you find out what works best.

It should go without saying that the words and phrases to be given such treatment must be carefully chosen. As a general principle, highlight the main benefits you are offering. Guarantees and incentives to act immediately should also be given extra emphasis. Another popular technique is to highlight the product name so that it leaps out at the reader, hopefully fixing it in his mind. However, forcing your product name down the reader's throat carries the risk of irritating him.

Length

Sales letters can be as long as necessary to tell your story. If you need four or six pages to do justice to it, then that is the length you should write to. But bear in mind that for business people time is money, so if possible it is sensible to avoid putting them off with multi-page epics. Householders usually have more time, and may be more responsive to long letters.

One other point is that most people tend to overwrite initially. So before you assume that your letter has to be six pages long, go over it carefully first looking for ways in which it could be trimmed down, cutting out long words and sentences, removing repetitions, and so on. If available, show your letter to a trusted friend or associate; a fresh pair of eyes will often see further cuts which could be made.

Postscript

Postscripts may be frowned upon in general business correspondence, but used carefully in sales letters they can be a powerful asset. Studies show that people tend to read a postscript before they have even read the letter itself. Use your postscript for a good purpose: to re-emphasise your strongest benefit, or emphasise why the reader should respond to your offer now.

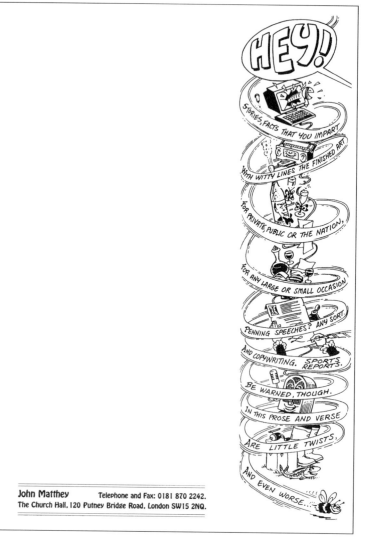

Figure 4. If you want to be noticed, get a letterhead that stands out! Freelance writer John Matthey commissioned a cartoonist to produce his, based on a verse he provided. He says, "It was the best £90 I've ever invested as it never fails to provoke a comment, and it puts me way ahead of the rest".

FINALLY...

Sales letters are a form of advertising neglected by many small businesses, yet in many cases they have the potential to increase their turnover at relatively little cost. In this chapter we have mainly been concerned with letters alone; the next chapter, looks at their role in the wider field of direct response.

'You cannot bore people into buying your product. You must interest them into buying it. You cannot save souls in an empty church.'

David Ogilvy - British advertising executive

KEY POINTS

- Sales letters have many uses. They can be sent to existing and former customers, enquirers, prospects identified from directories and list brokers, and so on.
- A good sales letter follows the AIDA specification. It attracts ATTENTION, arouses INTEREST, stimulates the DESIRE to purchase, and prompts ACTION.
- Many sales letters begin with an arresting headline. This grabs the prospect's attention and entices him to read on.
- The opening of the letter needs to make clear the main benefit being offered. It should answer the (implied) question, 'What's in this for me?'
- The letter should go on to explain and describe the product from a prospect's point of view.
- As well as describing the product, the letter should provide some evidence to back up your claims about it. This might include scientific evidence, reviews, quotes from satisfied customers, and so on.
- The end of the letter should prompt the reader to take action (fill in a form, phone your number, send for a full information pack, etc.). This is also the place to include an incentive for the reader to act immediately.
- Sales letters should use mainly short words, sentences and paragraphs. This gives pace and improves readability.
- Slang, jargon and abbreviations should be regarded with suspicion, and removed (or explained) if you believe that some readers will not understand them.
- Aim for a conversational tone which is friendly but factual. Avoid hype and advertisers' clichés ('this amazing offer').
- Most of the time, use the active rather than the passive voice.
- Use connecting words and phrases such as 'in fact', 'however', and 'on the other hand' to help your writing flow.
- Don't be afraid to use vertical lists where they will make information easier to take in.
- Use plain, simple punctuation: plenty of full stops, but other punctuation marks in moderation and only where they are required.
- Take time - as much as possible - to revise and polish your work.
- Devote some attention to the design of your letterhead. Take advantage of its potential as an advertising medium.
- Aim to personalise sales letters. If this is not possible, use a friendly salutation such as 'Dear Colleague' rather than the brusque and formal 'Dear Sir or Madam'.
- In longer letters, consider using sub-headings to help break up text on the page.

- Use the many forms of emphasis (underlining, emboldening, colour, etc.) to highlight important information such as main customer benefits and (perhaps) your product name.
- Sales letters can be as long as needed to tell your story. Aim for conciseness, however, especially if writing to business people where time is at a premium.

CHAPTER SIX

DIRECT RESPONSE

Direct response is more than just a form of advertising. It is in fact a method of marketing which by-passes the traditional retailer. Sales are made directly from producer to purchaser, via mail order, telephone selling or some other method. Direct response is the fastest-growing form of marketing in the UK.

WHAT SELLS THROUGH DIRECT RESPONSE?
A huge range of products and services is sold via this medium. They include:

- Insurance.
- Savings schemes.
- Pensions.
- Books.
- Computer programs.
- Business opportunities.
- Magazine subscriptions.
- Health plans.
- Hobby items.
- Electronic equipment.
- Educational products.
- Diet plans and health foods.
- Training seminars and correspondence courses.
...and more

Large mail order companies such as Littlewoods and Great Universal Stores can sell almost anything through their catalogues, but smaller companies are more restricted in what they can successfully offer. The best products/services for selling by direct response tend to have the following characteristics:

Unusual

The product cannot easily be found in high street shops, perhaps because it is a minority interest (e.g. model trains) or it is made to order.

Easily packaged

The product can be packed and posted without undue difficulty. This tends to exclude unusually shaped items, very heavy items, and those which are brittle or delicate.

Does not need to be demonstrated

The customer can be shown enough in the advertising material to convince him to buy. He does not need to see the product for himself. Even so, it may be wise to offer an unconditional money-back guarantee if the product does not meet the customer's requirements.

Fulfils a genuine need

A ready market exists for the product. On seeing the advertising material, recipients should be saying, 'Oh yes, I could do with one of those.'

Proven product

The product itself should be reliable and meet all the claims in your advertising. If it does not, you will swiftly find yourself engulfed by a tide of complaints and returns.

Attractive price

Ideally, the product should be available more cheaply through yourself than via other outlets (though it is wise to avoid relying on a lower price as your main selling point).

A good profit margin

Although in direct response there is no wholesalers' or retailers' mark-up to consider, advertising and related costs can be considerable. Experienced operators look for products that they can sell for at least three times the cost of the item to them. Advertising and promotion takes up another third of the asking price, leaving a final third for profit.

'Advertising can't sell any product; it can only help to sell a product the people want to buy.'

Jeremy Tunstall - British writer

DIRECT MAIL

Direct mail is the advertising medium most commonly used in direct response (though direct mail is not limited to direct response - for example, a retailer could use direct mail to attract customers into his shop). A direct mail campaign - commonly known as a mail shot - involves sending advertising material through the post to potential customers. The effectiveness of a mail shot depends on two things:

1. The accuracy of your mailing list.
2. The impact of what you have included.

MAILING LISTS

For a successful mail shot, an accurate mailing list is essential. Writing to people who have gone away, gone out of business, died, or are not interested in your product or service is a waste of time and money. There are various methods of obtaining a suitable list.

Your own files

The best, and cheapest, way of building up a mailing list is to start with your current or former customers. People who have enquired about your products or services should also be included. Even if they haven't yet bought anything, they are likely to be good prospects for the future.

Yellow Pages and other telephone directories

Yellow Pages can be an excellent source of business names and addresses. If you plan a mail shot outside your own area, most large libraries keep copies covering the whole country (as do Main Post Offices). Another good source is Thomson's Local Directory. These cover all of London and the South-East, and the main urban areas in other parts of the country (though not Northern Ireland). Finally, if you plan to mail local businesses, don't forget the directory produced by your local Chamber of Commerce.

The Electoral Roll

The electoral roll is a list of all adult voters in an area, street by street, house by house. It can be consulted in the main library covering the area, or at the council offices. The electoral roll can be a useful way of identifying people who live on their own (which might be relevant to an introduction agency) or single parents (if you have a special offer to make to them).

Professional directories

Most professional associations produce directories of their members. These list names and addresses, professional qualifications, fields of interest, and so on. If you want to write to public relations officers, for example, the Institute of Public Relations produces an annual handbook with register of members (published by Kogan Page). Copies of professional directories should be available in your main library, or you can order a copy direct from the association concerned. Even if the association doesn't publish a directory, they are certain to have a list of members which they may agree to sell you.

Rent (or buy) a mailing list

Many businesses supply mailing lists, either as a spin-off from their own marketing activities, or as their core business. If you buy a list you can use it as often as you like, but lists are seldom sold outright. More often you will have to rent, which means you are allowed to use the list a limited number of times only (though if any of the people you mail become customers you can add them to your own list and mail them as many times as you wish).

To prevent cheating, rented lists are 'seeded' with people known to the list owner. If these people receive more than the agreed number of mailings from you they will alert the list owner, who may then take action against you for breaching the rental agreement.

List brokers can supply mailing lists in a wide range of categories, usually for rental. Lists available include everything from single people to over-sixties, art collectors to vegetarians, business opportunity seekers to millionaires! Addresses of mailing list brokers can be obtained from the Direct Marketing Association (DMA), Haymarket House, 1 Oxendon Street, London, SW1Y 4EE (Tel. 020 7321 2525). This information is also available from the DMA website at www.dma.org.uk.

For business names and addresses, the largest company of all is Dun & Bradstreet. Their lists cover over 300,000 businesses, classified according to location, turnover and business type. Lists can be rented or bought, and are updated monthly. For more information contact: Dun and Bradstreet, Holmers Farm Way, High Wycombe, HP12 4UL (Tel. 01494 422000). If you decide to rent (or buy) a mailing list, try to find out as much about it as you can. Ideally, you need to know:

- How was the list compiled?
- Are the people on it buyers or simply enquirers?
- If buyers, how much did they spend, and on what?
- How old is the list?
- In what form will the names be provided (list of names? sticky labels? computer disk?)

Prices of lists vary widely, but between £30 - £100 (or more) per thousand names is typical. Recently compiled lists and lists of actual buyers rather than enquirers are more expensive but usually produce better rates of response.

Exchange mailing lists

You could also consider exchanging mailing lists with other non-competing businesses. This has the advantage of low cost, though identifying suitable businesses to exchange with may prove tricky. The key here is to envision your typical customer and ask what other products he might also want or need. For example, if you sell golfing accessories, you might suggest exchanging lists with a publisher of golf course guides.

Use a mailing house

There are over 200 mailing houses in the UK. While some are only interested in big business, many also cater to the needs of smaller operators. Mailing houses will take on a wide range of tasks, from writing and designing your mailshot, to printing it, to stuffing the envelopes, to franking them and sending them off to the post office. Different mailing houses specialise in different fields. To find the one best suited to your needs, speak to the Royal Mail's Postal Sales Representative for your area. Another good source of information is the Direct Marketing Association (contact details as above).

Use someone else's mailing

Alternatively, you could pay to have your material included in someone else's mailing. There are many possibilities here. For example, you could contact your local water or electricity company and see if they will accept your advertising material with their bills. Or, on a more local level, you could contact other non-competing businesses and see if they would be interested in taking your material in their own mailings in exchange for a contribution towards postage. Turning this on its head, you could ask if other businesses would like to advertise - for a price - in one of your own mail shots, thus cutting down on your overheads. With a little imagination, there are many ways in which this method could be applied.

THE DATA PROTECTION ACT

Bear in mind that if you keep details of individuals on a computer database, even if it is only their names and addresses, you will be legally obliged to register with the Data Protection Registrar. This involves filling in various forms explaining what information you keep on your database and what you use it for. There is also a small fee. Further information and registration forms are available from The Office of the Data Protection Registrar, Wycliffe House, Water Lane, Wilmslow, Cheshire, SK9 5AF (Tel: 01625 545745; Web: www.dataprotection.gov.uk/dprhome.htm).

WHAT SHOULD A MAIL SHOT INCLUDE?

There has been a trend in direct marketing for mail shots to become bulkier. The reasoning behind this is that most people, when they receive a mail shot, will look at every item in it, however briefly. It follows that the more items you include, the more opportunities you have to persuade your prospect to buy. A mail shot should normally include at least four items. These are:

1. Sales letter.
2. Leaflet or brochure.
3. Order form.
4. Return envelope.

Your aim is to provide all the information needed to persuade a prospect to order, and to make the actual mechanics of doing so as easy as possible. A separate order form and envelope (preferably reply-paid) obviously assist as far as the latter is concerned. The leaflet or brochure enclosed will be the one you use for general advertising purposes. If possible, include illustrations of your product in action.

The most important item in a mail shot is the sales letter, as this is where you set out the benefits you have to offer and ask for the order. At a pinch you could omit any or all of the other items, but the letter - your salesman in print - is crucial. Sales letters were discussed in detail in the last chapter, and the principles set out there apply when they are used in direct mail as well.

Other items which can be added to your mailshot as appropriate include testimonials, 'case studies', samples, free gifts, competitions, money-off vouchers, and so on. These can all help capture your prospect's attention and persuade him to buy. Watch your costs, however, and in particular check that the added weight of enclosures does not push the postal costs up a step.

PERSONALISATION

One point you need to consider is whether to personalise your mail shot for each recipient. Unless you are talking about very small numbers, the only practical way of doing this is with a computer. Modern word processors and desktop publishing (DTP) programs include the facility to incorporate information from a mailing list or database into a standard letter. This means that each letter in a mail shot can be personally addressed to the recipient (e.g. 'Dear Mrs Johnson' rather than 'Dear Sir/Madam'). You can also, if you wish, incorporate specific information about the recipient into the letter, such as their age or the road on which they live...as long as you have all this information on your database in the first place.

Research shows that personalising a mail shot can increase the response rate, but against this must be set the additional costs and time involved. In addition, with many large companies now routinely using this device, it may have lost some of its novelty value, and hence its effect. Also, the more personal information you include in a mail shot, the greater is the risk you will offend the recipient by getting some of it wrong. If you decide to go down this path, therefore, you will need to take great pains to ensure that the information in your database is accurate and up-to-date.

Ideally, the answer may be to compare the results achieved with personalised and non-personalised mail shots in small-scale test mailings. You should then have a much better idea whether or not it is worthwhile personalising the main mail shot.

PRESENTATION

In the field of direct mail you are competing with large companies such as Reader's Digest, insurance companies, book clubs, catalogue shopping companies, and so on. These businesses spend vast amounts on writing and designing their mail shots, and the end results generally appear highly polished and professional. While as a small business you do not necessarily need to match their best efforts, it is important that your mail shots are attractively designed and give a favourable first impression.

One thing which often lets down newcomers to direct mail is the envelope. It can be tempting to save money by using cheap manilla, but this is nearly always a mistake. People associate such envelopes with bills, circulars, official letters and 'junk mail'. It is better to spend a little more on good quality white envelopes, which people tend to associate with 'good' news. Window envelopes which reveal the recipient's address on the letter inside are acceptable and save you the trouble of writing the address on the envelope or using labels. You could also have envelopes printed with a message, or your business name/logo (if you think people will be encouraged to open the letter).

You can either assemble the mail shot yourself or use a mailing house (discussed earlier in the chapter). If you are doing it yourself, remember that people read the material on the inside and outside first, so put your letter at the front, your brochure at the back, and the order form and reply-paid envelope in the middle.

DISTRIBUTION

To distribute your mail shot, you will almost certainly need to use the services of the Royal Mail. A wide range of services is available for bulk mailers to assist them and help their budgets go further. Some of the most useful to small businesses are listed below (prices correct at time of writing).

Business collection

If you spend over £15,000 a year on postage, the Royal Mail will collect your post from your premises free of charge. Even if you do not spend this amount, they will collect for a fee. This is £420 a year for a daily collection from Monday to Friday, or just £210 if you agree to have your post collected before 3 p.m. A single, one-off collection of 1,000 items or more, or items with more than £200 postage value, is free. A single collection of fewer than 1,000 items, or items with less than £200 postage value, costs £5.

Mailsort

This title covers a range of services which provide discounts ranging from 13% to 32% for bulk mailings (over 4,000 letters or 1,000 packets at a time). Items have to be pre-sorted by the customer according to postcode, but Royal Mail provides help and advice on what is required.

Business Reply and Freepost

These services allow customers to contact you at your expense. With the Business Reply service, specially printed cards or envelopes (either first or second class) are supplied for customers' use. Business Reply is a good choice when using mail shots or magazine inserts to advertise.

With Freepost (second class only), customers reply by putting your Freepost address on their own envelopes. This can be ideal if you want to encourage a good response to TV, radio or press advertising, but you can also use your Freepost address on printed reply cards or envelopes in mail shots. There is an annual licence fee of £57 covering both these services. You then pay an additional 0.5p per item handled.

Private box

A private box provides you with a short and easy to remember alternative business address (e.g. PO Box 321). It can be useful if your postal address is on the lengthy side, or if you are operating from home but don't want customers and others to know this.

Mail posted to a private box is held at the local delivery office until you pick it up, or you can pay an extra fee to have it delivered to your usual address. A private box costs £52 a year or £42 for a half-year if you collect the mail yourself. If you want it delivered you pay the same amount again - giving a total cost in this case of £104 a year or £84 a half-year.

Household delivery service

The Royal Mail provides a door-to-door delivery service for leaflets, special offers and other promotional material. You can select the addresses to be delivered to according to a wide range of criteria. These include: postcode area, district or sector; TV region; geo-demographic (i.e. certain types of property only); residential/business, and so on. Costs vary according to the number and weight of items you are sending. Prices range from £28 to £53 per 1,000.

Admail

Admail allows you to have mail redirected. You can use this service if you wish to use a more prestigious address in your advertising, or if you want all replies to a particular advertisement to be sent somewhere else (e.g. a fulfilment house). Your Admail address can be short and therefore memorable, which is useful if you want to use it in advertising. All letters are redirected by first class post. Costs range from £100 for 30 days up to £600 for a year.

Franking

If you intend to send out regular mail shots, a franking machine may be a good investment. It will save you a lot of time and trouble buying and sticking on stamps, and the results look more professional. Alternatively, if you have a one-off mailing of at least 500 letters or packets you can take them to a Main Post Office and pay the standard postage in a lump sum. The Royal Mail will then frank the letters for you and deliver them in the normal way.

The Direct Mail Information Service

The Direct Mail Information Service (DMIS) undertakes regular in-depth research into the direct mail industry in the UK. You can get free outline reports from DMIS on topics such as direct mail trends, customer loyalty, response rates to mailshots, and so on. More information is available from The Direct Mail Information Service, 5 Carlisle Street, London, W1V 6JX (tel. 020 7494 0483). They also have a website at www.dmis.co.uk.

For more information about any of the above services, a good starting point is one of the Royal Mail sales or customer service centres found in most large towns and cities (look in the phone book under 'Royal Mail'). Take a look also at the Royal Mail website www.royalmail.co.uk.

TESTING YOUR MAIL SHOT

Large mail shots can be costly, especially if they do not pull in orders. It is therefore important to test your mailings in a small way before committing yourself to a large campaign. For small businesses, the best approach may be to begin by writing to existing customers with special offers and so on. If this proves successful, try mailing other potential buyers as well, but be very cautious before spending large amounts. If you are using a new, untried mailing list, start with a small test mailing - two or three hundred letters perhaps - and only try a larger number if the response to the test mailing proves encouraging.

RESPONSE RATES

The response rate is the proportion of people receiving your mail shot who respond to your offer. Response rates are usually measured in percentages. There are no hard and fast rules concerning what constitutes a good or bad response to a mail shot: one per cent or less can still be acceptable, so long as the product itself is sufficiently profitable. A typical average response rate to a targeted mailing is 2%; anything over 10% is exceptional.

Your main aim, in sending out your first mail shot, should be to cover all your costs and make a modest profit. The main profits from direct mail come not from the initial mailing but from subsequent mailings to people who buy from you. If a customer has bought from you once and been pleased with his purchase, there is every chance he will buy from you again.

FULFILMENT

Fulfilment means responding to replies to your mail shot. It is important to plan for this, and be prepared to respond promptly. If the aim of your mail shot is generate leads, for example, you

1

The perfect work-from-home
second income opportunity . . .

DOUBLE FREE BONUS

Mags To Riches

How you can turn every magazine and newspaper you
find into cash

Looking for a sensible way to earn money from home - without getting
ripped off? Look no further.........

An amazing new manual, Mags to Riches, shows how ANYONE can generate
high spare-time earnings from any of the 28 projects included. One project
needs only a handful of magazines or newspapers and a few household
accessories. Just think what you could do with an extra £100, £200, even
£1000 a week - the harder you work, the more you will earn.

Some of these projects will earn you a regular weekly income, others
could make you rich. Maybe very rich indeed.

The author, Avril Harper, has, as you would expect, already started
earning from some of these secrets herself, and the reason she is prepared to
divulge them to you is because there are far more opportunities than she can
ever hope to profit from herself.

The results are staggering. After several months researching her book,
looking for a handful of ideas to offer you, she suddenly found her new
findings had mushroomed to include dozens of ideas: some part-time, a few
spare-time, many full-time. More than this, the manual is filled with
illustrations, showing you what to watch out for and step-by-step instructions
about what to do next.

Quite simply, you can make money from almost everything you read and
this manual details how you can employ different techniques to get cheques
pouring through your letter box. It really doesn't matter what publication
you have, or how old it is, every single page is an earning source for you.

Some of these projects involve really old publications, the kind you'll
pay pennies for at jumble or car boot sales. Others use current magazines and
/...

2

Avril Harper - author of "Mags To
Riches". Editor of "Homeworkers Post"
and Winners Way".

Since 1990 Avril has run many successful
homebased businesses and is perhaps
Britain's most prolific money-making
ideas writer.

newspapers, which you can obtain thousands of
at no cost to you.

Here's how it's done

- You start any of these profitable
  projects without any risk
  whatsoever......there is no investment
  involved.

- Every project included in the manual can
  be run from the comfort and privacy of
  your own home.

- Get paid £5, £20 ... even £100 or more
  from every customer.

- Work when you want ... mornings, evenings
  or weekends - you choose the time and the
  place.

- No personal contact is required ...
  everything is done by mail.

• Included absolutely free of charge is a directory of professionals who
  will buy regularly from you .. they need YOU because they cannot afford
  to employ staff all over the world to carry out the few simple tasks
  most of these projects involve.

• There is nothing else to buy. This manual is all you need to get
  started.

This is an overview of what you will find in the manual

- How to get 1000's of people to pay for
  advertisements you cut out from every
  magazine you find.

- How to send the same clipping to
  hundreds of people without changing a
  word ... and how to make them want
  more of the same thing, in fact, as
  much as you can lay your hands on.

- How to send the same clipping to
  thousands of newspapers all over the
  world without changing a word. What
  to look out for, how to prepare it,
  how and who to send it to.

- How to earn a fortune from classified
  ads.

- How to earn hundreds of pounds a day
  as a writer without previous writing
  experience ... and where 15 minutes or
  so is all you have to spare.

- What Ken Dodd might buy from you.

- Discover what Sherlock Holmes couldn't
  find out for himself. And how it can
  earn you big money.

DON'T JUST TAKE OUR WORD ...

"Many thanks for "Mags To Riches".
Smashing! I was able to start one of
the projects the same day I received
the manual and another one over the
weekend."

R.K. Wirral

"Your book has hit the nail right on
the head as far as the home business
and extra income opportunity market
is concerned and I am pleased to
verify the book's worth for anyone
who is looking for a genuine, easy,
convenient and pleasurable way to
earn some additional income in their
spare time."

P.W. Berwick-upon-Tweed

"The book itself is excellent. It is
very thorough and full of wonderful
ideas for anyone wishing to make
extra money."

L.D. Coventry

3.

- How to write a book and sell a
  million copies without writing a
  single word.

- Birthdays - we all have them -
  how to turn everyone's birthday
  into cash for you.

- What to package and sell at 1000%
  mark-up.

- Something every person in the
  world wants from you. Another
  great idea for you to franchise or
  sell through hundreds of agents
  all over the world.

- Cut, clip and post! Perform this
  simple task five times a day and
  wait for the cheques to pile
  through your letter box.

- How to turn a handful of ads for
  things you can no longer buy, into
  a powerful profit-generating
  machine.

- How to profit from information research.

- How a pair of scissors, a pot of glue and a few sheets of paper can earn
  you a fortune.

- Write short stories professional writers will envy.

- The freebie that's worth a fortune for you.

- Make millions from romantic fiction, even without previous writing
  experience.

- What thousands of editors are desperate for but no-one's been able to
  give them. Until now.

Some of the secrets revealed have already generated massive incomes for
many, many ordinary people all over the world. Right now, there are extremely
few people operating any of these projects, in some cases none in this
country.

No special experience is called for on your part. You can operate as
many or as few of these projects as you like. However, we would recommend
anyone currently contemplating this "ground-floor" opportunity to do it now
... simply because if you don't establish a strong foothold in one or more
areas soon, someone else will beat you to it. Bear in mind that a few of
these projects are regional - only the earliest applicants will earn from
them.

What you might be surprised to see in the manual are literally hundreds
of contact names and addresses of actual people who'll want to keep on buying.
JUST ONE OF THESE ADDRESSES WILL KEEP YOU IN BUSINESS FOR YEARS.

One final thing. You can expect to earn £100, £200 up to £1,000 a week
and more from some of the projects revealed. Operate several and your
earnings can be as high as you want them to be. In fact, we are so convinced
you will generate a huge income from one, two, maybe all of these projects
that we are prepared to guarantee the manual unconditionally. Try "Mags to
Riches" at our expense and use the ideas for the next six months- if it fails
/...

FREE DOUBLE BONUS

● If you order within seven days
  you will save £5.00 - you will pay
  just £17.99 instead of the full
  price of £22.99!

● As a special thank you for
  ordering this manual, we will
  send you a FREE copy of
  "£150 in Ten Minutes". It's
  yours to keep regardless of
  whether or not you decide to
  return "Mags To Riches" for a full
  cash refund.

4

to live up to it's promise simply return the manual for a full cash refund.
We can afford to do this because we KNOW it's impossible for the book not to
work. There's something for everyone, regardless of abilities, qualifications
or experience and no matter how little or much time you can spare.

Order today and save £5.00 - here's how ....

The first print order is selling out fast and within a few weeks this
mailshot will have generated enough orders to exhaust current supplies. So
claim your copy of "Mags to Riches" TODAY. You can save £5.00 by mailing back
your Priority Reservation Form within SEVEN days. You pay just £17.99 instead
of the full price of £22.99. Why not take this first step straight away?

To claim your copy of "Mags to Riches" all you have to do now is simply
complete the enclosed PRIORITY RESERVATION FORM and return it direct to us.
But remember - you must order within 7 days to qualify for the £5.00 saving!

Yours sincerely,

Mike Chantry

Mike Chantry
Publisher

P.S. Remember there are dozens of great income-generating ideas for you to
benefit from. You only need one!

P.P.S.   As a personal "Thank You" for ordering the manual, we will send you
entirely FREE a copy of £150 in Ten Minutes. It's yours to keep even if you
decide to return "Mags to Riches".

P.P.P.S. By acting now you get a FREE list of 245 US names and addresses of
people waiting for you to contact them, and details of how to build an even
bigger mailing list, comprising many thousands, entirely FREE of charge - But
only if you are one of the first 100 people who orders "Mags to Riches".

Hilite Publishing, A division of Hilite Ltd. Registered in England No. 1988590.
Registered office: St James House, 8 Overcliffe, Gravesend, DA11 9LN

SPECIAL OFFER COUPON

HILITE LTD., ASH HOUSE, ASH ROAD, NEW ASH GREEN, LONGFIELD, KENT DA3 8SA.

YES! Please rush me a copy of "Mags To Riches".

☐ I am ordering within 7 days and therefore qualify for my £5.00 saving. I pay just £17.99.
I understand that if, after using the manual for 6 months, it fails to live up to your claims, I may return it for a full
cash refund, no questions asked.

Name (Mr/Mrs/Ms)
BLOCK CAPITALS PLEASE

Address

Postcode

☐ Cheque / P.O. enclosed, value £17.99, payable to 'Hilite Ltd' please

☐ Please debit my credit card £17.99 Access / Visa / Master Card   Expiry Date

Card No: [   ]   Signature

Date

PLEASE COMPLETE AND RETURN TODAY   SW 10 95

*Figure 5. Direct response advertising that packs a punch. Hilite's circular for Avril Harper's book 'Mags
to Riches' was sent to known business opportunity seekers in a successful mailshot. Notice, in particular,
the amount of 'you' copy, and the torrent of reader benefits.*

should aim to follow them up with a phone call within a day or two. If you are selling goods by mail order, you should try to turn them around the same day if possible. Delays create ill will, and reduce your credibility in the future.

Always take the opportunity to enclose something of additional interest with your fulfilment. For one thing, this is the cheapest advertising opportunity you will ever encounter. You might, for instance, enclose a list or catalogue of other products or services you supply, perhaps with a discount for the recipient as he is now a 'valued customer'.

Enclosing something extra is also a good - and inexpensive - opportunity to create customer goodwill. According to the nature of your product, you could enclose, 'Suggestions for Users', 'Hints on getting the best from...', a market research questionnaire ('What did you think of our product?), or even just a handwritten note saying, 'Thank you for your order'. It all helps generate goodwill and ensures that the customer comes back in the future, and recommends you to his friends and relatives.

FINAL THOUGHTS

Direct response, and in particular direct mail, is the fastest growing advertising medium in the UK today. Its popularity can only be ascribed to the fact that - done correctly - it works. The Royal Mail's 1994 Direct Mail Trends Survey revealed a number of interesting facts and statistics.

- The average person receives 1.7 pieces of direct mail every week.
- Two-thirds of people read their direct mail. 56% of those questioned said they had responded at some point, and 44% have made a purchase.
- Advertisers are taking more trouble to get personal details of recipients correct.
- The top three reasons people give for buying through the post are Convenience, Price and Not Available Elsewhere.

KEY POINTS

- Direct response is a method of marketing which by-passes the traditional retailer. Sales are made directly from producer to purchaser.
- Direct response is more suitable for some products and services than others. The best products to sell this way have a number of characteristics, including being unusual, easily packaged and not needing to be demonstrated.
- Direct mail is the medium most commonly used for direct response marketing. The effectiveness of a direct mail

campaign depends on two things: the accuracy of your mailing list, and the material you have included.

- The best mailing list consists of your own current and former customers, and people who have enquired from you even if they haven't yet bought anything.
- Yellow Pages and other directories (e.g. Thomson's) are a good source of business names and addresses.
- Other useful sources of addresses are the electoral roll and the directories or membership lists of professional associations.
- You can also rent (or buy) a mailing list. Lists are available from mailing list brokers, the largest of which is Dun and Bradstreet.
- If you decide to rent or buy a mailing list, try to find out as much as possible about how it was compiled.
- You can also exchange mailing lists with other retailers of non-competing goods.
- A mailing house will send out a mail shot on your behalf. Their services cover the entire process from designing the mailing to printing and sending it out.
- Another possibility is to pay to have your advertising material included in someone else's mailing.
- If you keep details of individuals on a computer database, you will need to register under the Data Protection Act.
- A mail shot should normally include at least four items: a sales letter, a leaflet or brochure, an order form and a return envelope. The most important of these is the sales letter.
- You will need to decide whether to personalise your mail shot to each recipient. This can increase its effectiveness, but may involve a lot more time and trouble.
- The mail shot must be well designed and presented to compete effectively with others. Avoid using cheap manilla envelopes.
- The Royal Mail offers a range of services which may be of interest to businesses using direct mail. These include business collection, Freepost and Business Reply Service, Mailsort, franking, and so on.
- Advice and information about direct mail is also available from the Direct Mail Information Service (DMIS).
- Before starting a major direct mail campaign, begin with a smaller test mailing to check the likely rate of response.
- Do not expect miracles from your first experiments with direct mail. A typical response rate to a targeted mailing is 2%, with anything over 10% exceptional.
- Be prepared to respond promptly to responses to your mail shot. Take the opportunity to enclose items of additional interest, e.g. advertising for other products and information/free gifts to create goodwill.

CHAPTER SEVEN

OTHER FORMS OF ADVERTISING

In this chapter - which is admittedly something of a rag-bag - I will be discussing a range of other advertising methods available to the small business. Some of these will be of interest only to a minority of small businesses, but let's start with one which is used by many...

LEAFLETS AND BROCHURES

Printed leaflets and brochures can carry more information than any newspaper or magazine advertisement. The message they convey can also last a lot longer. As most people will not bother to cut out and keep an advertisement, a newspaper ad will last only as long as the newspaper it is contained in; after a few days, at most, it will be thrown away. A well-designed and informative leaflet or brochure, by contrast, may be kept for future reference, perhaps for many months.

Brochures are small booklets. They normally consist of a few pages folded down the middle and stapled, perhaps with a card cover. Their most common uses are to send out to people enquiring about your services, perhaps in response to a newspaper advertisement. They may also be sent to existing customers or to people who have bought from you in the past. Brochures may include prices, or - to prevent them going out of date too soon - you may decide to insert a separate price list at the back. Brochures can be a cheap and cost-effective method of advertising, so long as they are distributed to people who are likely to have a genuine interest in buying from you.

Leaflets (sometimes referred to as handbills) are even simpler than brochures. They consist of just one or two pages, or perhaps a single page folded over. Because they are so cheap to produce, leaflets can be more widely used than brochures. They can be given out at exhibitions, used in mailshots, inserted in newspapers and magazines (for which you will, of course, have to pay a fee), dropped through people's letterboxes, or even handed out to passers-by in the street.

Although leaflets and brochures are inexpensive, their appearance should not detract from the image you are trying to project. So they should not look too cheap and tatty, and the style should be consistent with your letterhead and packaging. As with advertisements, the main message in a leaflet or brochure should concern the benefits of your product or service to the customer. Keep the style friendly and informal. Unless you are specifically aiming at technical people, avoid going into great technical detail. If such information is needed, it is normally better to keep the main text jargon-free and put product specifications, test data and so on in a separate section at the back.

When writing a leaflet or brochure, the same general principles apply as when writing an advertisement, though you can and should go into much more detail about your product. In addition, to achieve maximum effect, the design must be good. Many printers will advise and assist in preparing artwork for your leaflet or brochure, or for a higher quality (but more expensive) service you could try a commercial artist or graphic designer. Advertising agents will also undertake this work, although their charges can be high.

> *'There is no law which says that advertisements have to look like advertisements. If you make them look like editorial pages, you will attract more readers. Roughly six times as many people read the average article as the average advertisement...Very few advertisements are read by more than one reader in twenty. I conclude that editors communicate better than admen.'*

David Ogilvy - British advertising executive

ADVERTISING CARDS

Another option well worth considering is advertising cards. Postcard-sized ones can be put up in shop windows for a small price and can be very cost-effective for some kinds of business. Be prepared to spend a little time and money at the start having your cards professionally designed and printed.

You can also try using smaller advertising cards, similar in size to business cards (around 10 x 6 cm). These cards are very cheap to produce, and can be used in a variety of ways. They are particularly useful when advertising businesses such as fast food delivery or taxi services, which people may need at short notice. Cards can be left in hotels, restaurants, cafes, bars, telephone booths, shops, nightclubs and so on, either in small piles on a table or stuck to the wall (though it may be advisable to obtain the proprietor's permission first).

Small cards can also be put through people's letterboxes. Because of their handy size, people may be more inclined to put them in a purse or wallet for future use than they would with a leaflet. One idea which some firms have adopted is to print their own message on one side of the card, and on the other to include a list of phone numbers such as the local police, hospital, fire service, etc. The aim is to make the card a useful source of information for the recipient, so that it is more likely he will keep it for future reference.

BUYING PRINT

Whether you want brochures, leaflets or just plain business cards, at some point you will need to find a suitable printer and brief him on your requirements. Printers vary considerably in both price and quality, and it is a good idea to ask friends and business colleagues for their recommendations. Get samples and prices from several. Ask a few questions about their equipment and the kind of jobs they can do. Note whether they seem interested and enthusiastic, or bored and indifferent.

Having (hopefully) found a good printer, to get the best results it will help if you have some basic knowledge of printing techniques and processes. This is something you will soon pick up through experience, but in the early days don't be afraid to ask the printer and/or designer for his advice. In addition, free guides to various aspects of printing and communications are available from the marketing department of Kall Kwik Printing (UK) Ltd on 01895 872000.

To avoid any misunderstandings over an order, it is important to brief your printer so that he knows exactly what you require. Follow the checklist below.

- **TITLE** - give your order a title to help identify it, e.g. sales leaflet, promotional brochure.
- **QUANTITY** - make clear exactly how many copies you require. Bear in mind that, the more you order, the cheaper the price of

each individual item will work out. If in doubt get quotes for a number of different quantities (e.g. 500, 1,000 and 2,000) and see which will be most cost-effective.

- **FORMAT** - make clear exactly what format you require for each item: page size, number of pages and so on. The printer will be able to advise you as to what is most suitable.
- **COLOUR** - discuss with the printer or designer the colour/s you require. Items can be printed using one, two or three individual or 'spot' colours. Alternatively, by using a four colour process, you can produce materials with the full range of possible colours.
- **PAPER** - make clear what grade of paper you require. There is a wide variety of possible finishes (matt and gloss), colours and weights. Note that weight of paper is normally expressed in grams per square metre (gsm or g/m2). Ordinary typing paper is 80 gsm, while a high quality laid paper is 100 gsm or more. The printer will show you samples on request.
- **ARTWORK** - let the printer know exactly what format you will be supplying any artwork in. Photographs and illustrations normally have to be scanned to produce films and make plates from which to print.
- **PROOFS** - with complex jobs it is customary to request one or more proofs before the finished material is printed. This is in order to check that the item is as you envisaged, and give you an opportunity to put right any mistakes. Discuss with the printer at when proofs are required.
- **FINISHING** - print can be finished in a variety of ways, including varnishing, laminating, folding, stitching, collating, stapling, and so on. Discuss with the printer exactly what you require.
- **DELIVERY** - clarify where you want the finished goods to be delivered, or if you will be collecting them in person. Some printers will deliver orders above a certain value free of charge; others do not deliver at all.
- **SCHEDULE** - advise the date and time required for each proof stage and final delivery. Avoid simply stating 'as soon as possible', as this will simply ensure that your order goes to the back of the queue.
- **PAYMENT** - most high street printers will ask for payment on collection, but they may be persuaded to set up a monthly account once they can see that you are going to be a regular customer. Printers who deal more with trade customers than members of the public may allow you to pay on a 30 day invoice.

Although the emphasis throughout this book has been on getting value for money, this does not always mean choosing the cheapest options where print is concerned. Much depends on the kind of image you want your advertising to project. An up-market fitted kitchen company, for example, would certainly need a glossy brochure with full colour printing to present the desired image to potential clients. On the other hand, to announce the opening of a new shop or a summer sale, a simple, one-colour handbill may be quite sufficient.

TELEVISION

Television is the most expensive form of advertising, and for new small businesses other media such as local newspapers may be more appropriate. Nevertheless, the independent television companies are increasingly able to offer local or at least regional advertising at a reasonable price, and as your business grows it is certainly an option you may wish to consider.

A TV advertising slot is generally very short: there is seldom time to state more than the main user-benefit and how viewers can obtain your product. To make the best use of the time available, a highly professional approach is needed. Channel Four are said to be very helpful to first-time advertisers. However, if you are considering TV advertising, it is probably best to go through an advertising agency rather than attempt to do it all yourself.

RADIO ADVERTISING

Commercial radio stations offer widespread coverage for a reasonable cost, and are becoming increasingly popular as advertising media. A surprisingly wide range of goods are advertised this way. They include:

- Insurance.
- Food products.
- Sports goods.
- Furniture shops.
- Mobile phones.
- Soft drinks.
- Restaurants.
- Films/videos.
- CDs.
- Books.
- Garages.
- Health Clubs.

To be effective, radio advertisements need to repeated many times. The listener profile varies widely throughout the day: peak time is early morning, while people are preparing to go to work. By mid-morning there is a much smaller audience consisting mainly of housewives and retired people. It is therefore very important to ensure that your advert is running at times of day when members of your target market segment are likely to be listening.

For small businesses, the most likely starting point will be your local independent commercial radio station. In London this might be Capital Radio; in Birmingham, BRMB; in Manchester, Piccadilly; and so on. There is also an increasing number of national commercial radio stations, e.g. Virgin Radio and Classic FM. The latter are worth considering if you are selling to a nationwide market, and the station's listener profile matches your own target market segment.

Most commercial radio stations have advertising departments which will write and record your advertisement for you at low or no cost. They generally have no objection to your using the advertisement on other radio stations as well as their own. If radio advertising is of interest to you, contact the advertising manager at your local radio station for a preliminary discussion.

CINEMA

A few years ago it seemed that TV and video would spell the end for cinemas, but in recent times they have made a come-back. Giant multi-screen complexes, showing as many as twenty different films simultaneously, have been opening mainly in out-of-town locations across Britain (though admittedly often at the expense of small local picture houses).

As an advertising medium, the cinema has a number of attractions for small businesses. In particular, it is possible to advertise in cinemas in your local area only, or even in just a single cinema. This means that this form of advertising can work out surprisingly economical. You can also specify exactly when you want your advertising to be shown (e.g. a swimwear company could book its advertisement to run for four weeks in the early summer).

Advertising slots of 20, 30, 40 or 60 seconds are normally available, and there may also be special, shorter slots for local businesses. The cost of producing a cinema advertisement can be high, but the main advertising contractors (Rank Screen Advertising and Pearl & Dean) have stock footage suitable for a wide variety of businesses, to which your own details can be added at the end.

Defining whom exactly your advertising will reach can be difficult, as so much depends on the film showing. The audience for a French Art House film will be very different from that of the latest Mel Gibson blockbuster, and this will be different again from the audience for a Walt Disney family cartoon. The main age group which regularly visits the cinema, however, is 15-24 year olds. If this corresponds with your target market segment, cinema could offer a cost-effective way of getting your message across to them.

To find out more about cinema advertising ask the manager of your local cinema if he will put you in touch with the advertising contractor's local sales representative.

TRANSPORT ADVERTISING

This is another form of advertising well worth considering if you are operating within a local geographical area. Buses and trains are the main options here. Buses offer three main areas for advertising:

1. The side panels.
2. The rear panels.
3. Interior.

Side panels are the largest and most obviously visible, and can provide a way of putting your business name up alongside those of nationally-known companies. For small businesses, however, they are not cheap. The rear panels of buses are seen mainly by other drivers, and therefore tend to be most suitable for businesses such as garages and car part dealers.

For the average small business, the best choice of advertising in buses is the interior. There are two main areas where you can advertise: the front bulkhead and the roof panels. Such advertisements have to be fairly small, but they are viewed by a captive audience, many of whom may be on their way shopping. Clearly, therefore, the best routes on which to advertise are those which pass near your premises. Most bus advertising is handled by one of three companies:

1. Primesight, which handles bus advertising in cities outside London.
2. London Transport, which handles advertising in the Greater London area.
3. British Transport Advertising, which handles advertising in buses which run between cities.

For more information, contact the local sales office of the relevant contractor. All three will design and print your posters or cards, put them up, and ensure that they are kept on display until your advertising time is up.

Trains offer similar opportunities to advertise, both internally and externally. You can also advertise in railway stations, in a range of poster sites both on the platform and in booking offices and waiting rooms. The majority of people travelling by train tend to be commuting to work, which means that this can be a good advertising medium for employment agencies, insurance and other financial services, and so on. Advertising in trains and stations is handled by British Transport Advertising; ask the station manager for contact details of their local sales representative.

'Good times, bad times, there will always be advertising. In good times people want to advertise, in bad times they have to.'

Bruce Barton - American advertising executive

LOCAL POSTER SITES

There are some 140,000 dedicated poster sites across the UK, in addition to the many other opportunities for poster advertising in railway stations, bus stops, ferry terminals and so on. The fact that you can buy poster advertising on one or more local sites, as well as regionally or nationally, makes this a form of advertising many small businesses may wish to consider.

The basic unit size for a poster is the double crown. This is a single sheet 20 inches wide by 30 inches high. The most widespread and popular size for advertising is the 16-sheet, with the 4-sheet also common in some locations. There are also larger 'super-sites' using 48 sheets and more, but the cost of booking these means that they are unlikely to appeal to the average small business.

Most poster sites are controlled by one of the four big contractors in this field. These are More O'Ferrall, Mills & Allen, London & Continental, and Maidens. They will put up your poster for you and look after it for the period you have paid, replacing it if it becomes damaged or defaced. Posters are normally booked for a month, but you can also arrange to have your poster displayed, "till countermanded", which means that the poster remains on display until you decide to cancel it.

Posters are highly visible, and can be good for keeping your name in the public eye. Their main drawback is that they are read by people on the move, so there is no time to spell out a detailed advertising message. You can book your advertising to run whenever you wish - assuming there is no prior booking on the site you require - but the contractors like to have the posters in their hands at least four weeks before they are due to go up.

If there is a particular site on which you would like to advertise, take a close look and you should find the name of the contractor displayed somewhere around it. There is likely to be a phone number for enquiries, or you should be able to get the number of the contractor's local sales office from the phone book or Directory Enquiries.

DIRECTORIES

Whatever other forms of advertising you use, don't neglect to advertise in Yellow Pages. As you will no doubt be aware, these are local telephone directories published by British Telecom covering the whole of the UK. There are also the independently produced Thomson's local directories, which cover London and South-East England and the main urban areas in other parts of the country (though not Northern Ireland). Research suggests that Yellow Pages are more widely used, even in households which have both.

Anyone who rents a business line is automatically entitled to an entry in their local Yellow Pages, but it is worth spending the relatively modest fee to have a semi-display or display advertisement. This will make your entry stand out from others in the same category, and is an opportunity to set out some of your main selling points. You might also find it worthwhile to pay extra to have your advertisement included in other Yellow Pages apart from your own local one.

There is no automatic right to a free entry in Thomson's Local Directory (though business line users may be included without charge 'at the publisher's discretion'), but again if you decide to advertise it is worth paying the extra to make your advertisement stand out. Thomson's national office is: Thomson Directories, Thomson House, 296 Farnborough Road, Farnborough, Hants, GU14 7NU (Tel. 01252 555555; Web: www.thomweb.co.uk).

Finally, there are a large number of trade directories, yearbooks, etc. which accept advertising. Care must be taken, however, as these are often highly priced and sell only a small number of copies. If at all possible speak to people in the trade you hope to sell to, and find out which directories they actually use.

THE INTERNET

In the last few years there has been an explosion of interest in the Internet, with businesses falling over themselves to grab a place in what is now generally acknowledged to be the advertising medium of the future. So how relevant is the Internet to the average small business?

Let's begin with the most fundamental question: what is the Internet? It is basically a world-wide network of interconnected computers. The Internet began in the USA and is still US dominated, but it is not under the control of any particular government or agency. Anyone with a computer and a modem (a device which enables a computer to communicate with others via an ordinary phone line) can link up and gain access to the information stored on many thousands of computers across the world.

The part of the Internet used by most businesses to advertise - and sometimes sell - their wares is the World Wide Web (or Web for short). The Web is the most technologically sophisticated part of the Internet; it allows users to display full colour graphics, video clips, animations and so on, as well as text. Viewers can move quickly and easily from one Website to another via so-called hyperlinks. The usual procedure for advertisers is to create a Home Page which gives readers information about their product/service, and some means of contacting and (perhaps) ordering from them.

Creating a basic Home Page for your business is actually quite straightforward, with most IAPs (Internet Access Providers) including free Web space as part of their overall service package. IAPs also in most cases provide the basic software (tools) needed to create a page suitable for publishing on the Web. Obviously it takes a little time to master the techniques involved, but with modern Website creation software most of the actual 'programming' is done automatically. All you have to do is design your page, much as you might design a leaflet or brochure, and the software then does the rest of the job for you.

If, despite this, you do not want to create a Home Page yourself - or you fancy something more ambitious, perhaps including the facility to take orders online - various firms will do this for you for a fee. Check in Yellow Pages under Internet Providers & Services. As a general principle, it is important that Web advertising is both entertaining and informative. People who are 'surfing' the World Wide Web have a huge range of sites they can visit; if yours does not grab their interest, they will swiftly move on somewhere else.

Getting people to visit your Website requires some planning and effort. One method is to include your URL (Uniform Resource Locator - your Web address) in your conventional advertising. Another method is to ensure that your site is linked with others. For example, most people use so-called Search Engines to find their way around the Web. Users can enter a key word or words, and the Search Engine will then direct them to a number of relevant sites. By contacting the Search Engine operators you can ensure that anyone searching for 'window cleaners' or 'Indian restaurants' (to give two randomly chosen examples) is referred to your site.

One problem which has slowed the growth of the Web as a

marketing medium has been concern among users about the security implications of giving out their credit card details over the net. However, encryption methods have been developed to ensure that people can enter such information with little risk of it being intercepted, and it appears that this problem is well on the way to being solved.

For some types of business, it is likely that the Internet will transform the way that they work. For others - such as small local retail and service businesses - its impact may be less. Where advertising is concerned these are still early days; but with its potential for contacting many millions of potential buyers across the world at a cost of literally a few pounds a month, the Internet offers possibilities few businesses will wish to ignore completely. A useful guide for newcomers to the net is 'The Internet for Dummies' by John Levine and Carole Baroudi (IDG Books). Seminars and courses on the Internet are run by The Marketing Guild, 1 Houghton Court, Houghton Regis, Dunstable, Beds, LU5 5DY (Tel. 01582 861556; Web: www.marketing-guild.com). The Guild's associated company Internet Marketing Limited assists businesses in marketing themselves on the Internet.

KEY POINTS

- Leaflets and brochures have the advantages that they can carry more information than any printed advertisement, and if well designed may be kept for much longer.
- Brochures are small booklets, normally sent to people who have already expressed an interest in your product or service. They generally include a separate price list.
- Leaflets or handbills have just one or two pages. Being cheaper than brochures they can be used for a wide range of purposes, including mail shots, 'door stuffers', and so on.
- Advertising cards are a useful option for certain kinds of business, especially those which may be needed in a hurry. You could try printing useful phone numbers on the back to encourage people to retain them.
- Finding a good printer may require research. Find out from friends and colleagues whom they use. Visit them, and ask to see samples of their work.
- To avoid misunderstandings, make clear to the printer exactly what you require in any particular job. The considerations include quantity, format, colour, what proofs are required, payment methods and so on.
- Do not assume you must always choose the cheapest options where print is concerned. If you wish to project an up-market image, you must be prepared to spend more to achieve this.

- Television advertising is expensive, but companies are now making efforts to attract small business advertisers. If you are considering TV advertising, it is probably best to go through an advertising agency rather than attempt to do it all yourself.
- Radio advertising can provide widespread coverage for a reasonable cost, and is increasingly popular among small businesses. To be effective, radio advertisements need to be repeated many times.
- Commercial radio stations have advertising departments which will write and record your advertisement for you. Most have no objection to your using the advertisement on other radio stations as well as their own.
- Cinema is another potential advertising medium, especially if you wish to target the 16-24 age group. You can book an advertisement to run in your local area, or even just one local cinema.
- Buses and trains offer many opportunities for advertising. Bear in mind that many people on buses are going shopping, while on trains the majority are commuting to and from work.
- Local poster sites are another possible choice for advertisers. Posters are read mainly by people on the move, so the message needs to be kept short and simple.
- Every small business should advertise in Yellow Pages, and possibly in Thomson's local directories as well. A semi-display or display ad will make your advertisement stand out from the competition.
- Many other directories also take advertising. Care must be taken, however, as these are often highly priced and sell only a small number of copies. If possible find out from people in the relevant trade which directories they actually use.
- The Internet is a new advertising medium with great potential for some kinds of business. It is a world-wide network of interconnected computers. Anyone with a computer and a modem can gain access via the Internet to the information stored on many thousands of computers across the world.
- The part of the Internet most commonly used for advertising is the World Wide Web. Various agencies have sprung up which will create a Web 'Home Page' for you on which to advertise, and perhaps sell, your wares.
- If you decide to advertise on the Internet, you will need to think carefully about how to encourage people to visit your site, and how to keep their interest once they are there.

CHAPTER EIGHT

POINT-OF-SALE
AND EXHIBITIONS

Point-of-sale (POS) advertising is, quite literally, advertising at the point of sale - in other words, the place where the product or service can be obtained. By definition, this is frequently a shop, but it might also be:

- A market stall.
- An exhibition stand.
- A reception area.
- A waiting room.
- A sales department.
- An office open to the public.
- A workplace or site.

Good point-of-sale advertising attracts attention and provides customers with useful information at the place where purchases can actually be made. For businesses able to use POS advertising - it would obviously not be relevant to mail order companies, for example - it can provide a highly cost-effective means of boosting sales.

In this chapter I will be looking at POS advertising from two slightly different perspectives: first, from suppliers producing material for retailers who stock their products; and second, from the point of those in retail and other businesses, looking at how they can use POS advertising effectively on their own premises.

WHAT POS MATERIALS ARE THERE?

POS material comes in many different forms. The list below is by no means comprehensive:

- Posters.
- Stickers.
- Wall clocks.
- Open/closed signs.
- Leaflet displays.
- Mobiles (display devices which are suspended from the ceiling).
- Showcards.
- Models (e.g. a model aeroplane in a travel agent's).
- Cut-out figures (e.g. the swimsuited Kodak girl in shops offering photographic services).
- Dump-bins (tubs used to present a quantity of a particular brand).
- Dummy packs (empty packs, perhaps larger than normal size, for use in displays).
- Display boards and display stands.
- Dispensers (hanging cards from which small items such as combs, pens etc. can be pulled off).
- Display outers (boxes of small items such as bars of chocolate which, when opened up, can be used to display the goods inside).
- Sales literature of all types (leaflets, catalogues, price lists, etc.).

In addition, there are more specialised materials which can be used in particular types of business. In pubs, for example, drip mats, dart boards, ash trays and towels are all used for POS advertising. And manufacturers of computer products have not been slow to spot the potential for advertising on mouse mats.

Advertising may be described as the science of arresting the human intelligence long enough to get money from it.'

Stephen Leacock - British humorist

PROVIDING POS MATERIALS FOR RETAILERS

Retailers do appreciate POS materials, as they help them sell more of the product concerned. However, many are swamped with more material than they can use, much of which, as a result, lies around gathering dust in the stock room.

If you are thinking of producing POS material to support your

LEAFLETS

An effective way to boost your business!

* Black ink on selected papers.
* An illustration or your company logo.
* We have an extensive library of copyright free illustrations.

FOR ONLY

£39 A5 SIZE ONLY

for 1000

PRICE LIST

1,000 - £39	5,000 - £98	9,000 - £149
2,000 - £59	6,000 - £102	10,000 - £158
3,000 - £74	7,000 - £126	15,000 - £191
4,000 - £88	8,000 - £138	20,000 - £225

Prontaprint!

Yes we can. Yes we do.

1097 Warwick Road, Acocks Green, Birmingham, B27 6QT
Tel: 0121-708 2700   Fax: 0121-706 0870

Designed & Printed

Figure 6. This handbill was available from a dispenser near the till of the print shop in question. It is a good example of simple, but effective, point-of-sale advertising.

stockists, therefore, it is advisable to conduct some preliminary research to find out what they will find most useful. Visit retailers and ask for their views, and study the areas of the shop in which your material is likely to be displayed.

POS materials should be suitable for the environment in question. In supermarkets or grocers' shops, for example, your POS materials will be competing with many others, so they will need to be eye-catching to attract attention; showcards, mobiles and display stands may be among the best choices here. In a less competitive setting such as a pharmacy, leaflets and brochures, as long as they contain useful, relevant information, may be quite sufficient.

PRODUCING POS MATERIAL

Before producing special POS material, check to see whether any of your existing advertising material could be adapted for this purpose. As mentioned above, leaflets and brochures, price lists and advertising cards can all work well in the appropriate setting. It can also be a good idea to have a copy of your catalogue available for customers to consult. If you decide to provide material for people to take away, monitor stocks regularly and replenish them when needed.

Stationery shops and display material dealers can supply a range of POS units and receptacles, and they can also be made to measure by specialist display designers and manufacturers. You can have your business name or advertising message printed over them, or simply use them unprinted to hold POS material and keep it tidy.

DISPLAYS

Many businesses have to mount displays of their products. One of the most common is a shop window display, but displays are also needed in exhibitions, market stalls, craft fairs, and so on.

A good display will attract attention, emphasise certain features of the product, and put the customer in the right frame of mind to purchase. Creating a good display is an art rather than a science, but certain principles can be set out.

1. Displays should be brightly-lit to catch the eye.
2. Try to achieve a pleasing harmony by using colour, lighting and a variety of items.
3. When displaying mainly small products, create a number of levels by using plinths draped with material.
4. Displays are often more effective if the main item is placed not in the centre but slightly to one side, with other items in the display to balance it.
5. All articles on display should be clearly priced.
6. Window displays should be changed weekly or fortnightly, and have a theme (e.g. holidays, Christmas, autumn) or a common colour.
7. With large windows, use blinds or drapes to draw in the eye.
8. Avoid trying to cram too many items into small windows. Instead, change the display more often.

To get ideas, it is a good idea to look in the windows of the large department stores, all of whom employ professional window dressers. Take notes or even photographs, so that you can adapt their ideas in your own displays.

LIGHTING

Lighting has already been referred to above, but it is so important in creating the right atmosphere for selling that I make no apology for mentioning it again. For both practical and psychological reasons retail areas should be well-lit, preferably with at least some natural daylight. Ordinary light-bulbs and tubes tend to create a very even tone, with no highlights, shadows or pools of interest. Tracked spotlighting systems allow you to highlight displays and create a more interesting environment. Beware, however, the effects of heat from spotlights on books and perishable goods.

Fluorescent lights are a popular and economical choice in shops, but it is important to replace them as soon as they start to flicker, as many people find the effect offputting. In epileptics it can trigger a fit.

COLOUR

Choosing the right colour for displays and decor can play a major role in creating the atmosphere you want. Many colours have emotional associations, and it is worth bearing these in mind:

- Green   - natural, the countryside, the environment.
- Blue   - peaceful, cool, calm, reflective.
- Red   - danger, excitement, warmth.
- Brown   - country crafts, down-to-earth, honesty.
- Yellow   - the sun, bright, eye-catching.
- Purple   - stately, old-fashioned.
- Turquoise   - luxury, expensive.
- White   - pure, clean (but in large amounts can be cold and institutional).

Colours can appear quite different under different types, intensities and angles of lighting. It is worth experimenting with colour schemes and lighting until you get the effect you require.

PROPS

Props are used in window displays, where they can help to emphasise the subject or theme of the display. For example, a clothing shop with an autumnal theme for its display might include, along with seasonal clothing, a wheelbarrow full of fallen leaves and a broom. Props should not be allowed to dominate a display, simply to lend it added interest.

Props, or accessories, are also used in businesses such as pubs and restaurants, where they help to establish a theme and provide atmosphere. This is an area where you can allow your imagination free rein – but be wary of spending large amounts unless your market research has shown that customer response will justify this.

PRICE TICKETS

Few things can lower a business's image more effectively than tatty, or absent, price tickets. Many people do not like to ask the price, perhaps fearing that this will commit them to purchasing the product; and rather than try to decipher an illegible label, they will simply go elsewhere.

Ensure, therefore, that all products on display are clearly ticketed. Unless you have a good freehand script, use Letraset or a proprietary ticketing machine.

EXTERIORS

Just as important as the inside of your premises is the outside. The exterior is the first impression a visitor gets of your business, so it is important that it is well signed and kept clean. This applies whether your business is a shop, an office, a factory or a one-man building firm.

Various forms of point-of-sale material may be displayed outside a business's premises. They include:

- Posters.
- Billboards.
- Standing signs.
- Flags.
- Bunting.
- Banners.

Exterior signs and displays are controlled by local planning authorities through the Advertisement Regulations (part of the Town and Country Planning Acts). The following signs are exempt from these regulations:

1. A sign on the outside of the premises stating the business name and what you do. To avoid having to apply for planning permission, this must be below the first floor window sill. Letters and figures must not be more than 2'6" high.
2. If your premises have two frontages, you are permitted two signs.
3. A single flag-pole.

In designated Areas of Special Control (e.g. conservation areas) additional rules apply. For example, the maximum height of letters and numbers in premises signs is 1 foot.

'Advertising is found in societies which have passed the point of satisfying the basic animal needs.'

Marion Harper Jr - American advertising executive

OTHER OPPORTUNITIES FOR POS ADVERTISING

If your business has a van or other transport, don't neglect this opportunity for some free advertising. Get a professional signwriter to put on your business name, logo (if you have one), phone number and address, as well as the nature of the service or product you provide.

In addition, businesses which work on customer premises such as builders, decorators, landscape gardeners and so on are missing an excellent opportunity if they fail to put up advertising boards visible to passers-by. A builder friend finds that this form of advertising, combined with word of mouth (the best advertising of all), brings him enough customers without the need for any other kind of advertising.

HIGHWAY SIGNS

Although not strictly point-of-sale material, highway signs are an important form of advertising for some businesses, especially those heavily dependent on tourism and passing trade (country pubs, restaurants, transport cafes, etc.).

Most such signs need planning permission. Whether this is likely to be obtained depends on local council policies, whether residents object, and so on. In practice many highway signs do not have planning permission, and rely on local authorities turning a blind eye. In this regard, handwritten posters stating 'Fresh Strawberries Here Today' are reasonably safe, but more permanent-looking signs are likely to attract unwelcome attention. The safest option may be to find a friendly farmer who will allow you to put up a sign at the edge of his field.

EXHIBITIONS AND CONFERENCES

There are over 3,000 trade fairs and exhibitions every year in the UK alone, with many more overseas. From a businessman's point of view, an exhibition provides the chance to meet several hundred potential buyers over the space of a few days, compared with the five or six a day the average sales representative can visit. Hiring a stand at an exhibition is expensive, and requires careful planning if it is to be successful. To find out which exhibition might be most appropriate for your business, a good starting point is Exhibition Bulletin. This monthly guide costs £100 for a year's subscription or £35 for a single copy (prices correct at time of writing). For further details contact: Exhibition Buletin, 131 Southlands Road, Bromley, Kent, BR2 9QT (Tel: 020 8778 2288; Web: www.expobase.com/exbuhp.htm). Most shows are advised six months ahead.

Another, lesser-known option for small businesses and the self-employed is to exhibit at a conference. This is often much cheaper than attending an exhibition, though the potential audience will be limited to conference delegates. Nevertheless, if you can find a conference aimed at people in your target market segment, it can be highly effective.

For example, I recently attended a conference for school governors concerning the arts and education. In the communal area used during lunchtime and breaks, there was an exhibition of around forty stands representing individuals and organisations working in music, theatre-in-education, and so on. Far from paying, the exhibitors had been paid a fee for attending, on the basis that their presence would enhance the value of the conference for delegates. Such opportunities are not widely advertised, but you can mailshot likely organisations in your field explaining your interest and asking to be put on their mailing list.

ADVERTISING FOR THE EXHIBITION

Once you have decided to attend an exhibition, it is important to begin planning the advertising immediately. Newspapers and magazines often publish special features or whole issues connected with the exhibition, with advertising at special rates for exhibitors. Liaise with the exhibition organisers, who should know of any such plans.

All exhibitors should be entitled to a listing in the exhibition guide or programme, but it may be worth paying extra to advertise. If you do, be sure that your advertisement gives people some compelling reason to visit your stand. An advertisement which says little more than, 'Well, here we are' is likely to be a waste of money.

Most exhibitions are attended by the press, and this can be a good opportunity to gain some extra free media coverage. In particular, if you are launching a new service or product, be sure to bring along press releases, photographs and other background material, and leave copies in the exhibition's press room. This topic is further discussed in Chapter 11, Public Relations.

DESIGNING YOUR STAND

At an exhibition you may be competing with hundreds of other stands for attention, so it is important that yours appears both interesting and welcoming. Visual displays of all kinds catch the eye, especially those which involve movement. Demonstrations, working models, videos, slide shows, computer displays and so on can all be highly effective.

At the very least, you should have a set of well-designed and attractive display boards. Boards can be bought outright or hired. The most useful type to work on are those surfaced with brushed nylon, as you can stick things to these using Velcro tabs. A company which can supply a wide range of display boards is Marler Haley ExpoSystems Ltd, Little End Road, Eaton Socon, St Neots, Cambridgeshire, PE19 3SN (Tel. 01480 477373; Web: www.marlerhaley.co.uk). Below are a few basic principles for creating an effective display.

1. Be clear what you want your display to achieve. Is it to sell more product, launch a new line, find new distributors or agents, or some other purpose? A display should have no more than one key aim.
2. Plan your display. You should aim for consistency and balance. This can be achieved through various methods, including a matching colour scheme, symmetry, use of repeating elements (e.g. your logo) and so on.
3. Think big! Your display can use range of items, including photos, posters, maps, drawings, text and so on - but all should be as large as possible. Small photos with tiny captions will lose half your audience immediately.
4. Use photographs wherever possible. Photos are always an asset in displays. Ideally they should be eye-catching, colourful and show people doing something interesting (not just static photos of your product). Photos can be enhanced by mounting them on card.
5. Protect your display. Especially at a busy exhibition, your boards may have to put up with being fingered, brushed or even worse. Protect them by using a transparent film such as Coverseal, or a clear, spray-on varnish.
6. Provide material for people to take away. Ensure that there is a good supply of your leaflets or brochures near the display (ideally in a dispenser attached to it). Make sure this is prominently flagged with a sign saying, 'Please take one'.

ON THE DAY

Arrive early, giving yourself plenty of time to put up your boards and arrange your leaflets and brochures. Once visitors start to arrive, you (and your staff, if you have any) need to appear friendly and approachable. If a visitor is showing an interest in your stand, give them a few moments to get their bearings before going over to them (unless, of course, they approach you directly). Avoid opening with, 'Can I help you?' as this is likely to be met by, 'Just looking, thanks', leaving you in limbo. Instead try something like:

- 'Have you used our service before?'
- 'Which of our products were you most interested in?'
- 'This has just been launched at the show.'
- 'Let me show you how this works.'
- 'Are you in retail or wholesale?'
- 'The advantages of this are...'

If the visitor has no more than a casual interest, offer him a leaflet and leave him to browse. Your aim should be to concentrate on people who have a genuine interest in buying from you. Depending on the field you are in, you may be able to make some sales at the show, but it is more likely that you will use this opportunity to make an appointment to visit the prospect at his place of work some time in the next few weeks. This, of course, is when the real selling will take place.

An important aim in attending an exhibition is to get the names and addresses of potential customers you can follow up later. A good tactic with people you judge to be serious prospects is to ask for their details on the promise of sending them a full information pack in the post ('To avoid weighing you down with literature just now'). Another popular ploy is the free prize draw. To take part, all prospects have to do is place their business card in a box on your stand. This can be a good way of building or updating your mailing list, but has the drawback that some of those entering the draw will have little interest in actually buying from you.

When the exhibition is over, follow up any enquiries promptly, and evaluate the success or otherwise of your attendance. Exhibiting is an art all of its own, and you will undoubtedly learn lessons from every one you attend. For a more in-depth guide to making the most of exhibitions, see 'How to Make Exhibitions Work For Your Business' by John Talbot, a Daily Telegraph Guide published by Kogan Page.

KEY POINTS
- Point-of-sale (POS) advertising is, literally, advertising at the point of sale. This is often, though not always, a shop.
- Many different kinds of POS material are produced, but much of it is never used. It is important to check with stockists what form of POS material they would find most useful to support your product.

- Before producing special POS material, check whether existing material such as leaflets and brochures may be suitable for this purpose.
- You can obtain POS units and receptacles from stationery shops and display material dealers, and have them overprinted with your own message. You can also have POS material made to measure by specialist display designers and manufacturers.
- Businesses often have to create displays for shop windows, exhibition stalls, etc. A good display will attract attention, emphasise certain features of the product, and put the customer in the right frame of mind to purchase.
- Various principles which can be applied in creating a good display. These include ensuring that the display is brightly lit and harmonious. All goods for sale should be clearly priced.
- Shop window displays should be changed frequently and have a theme or a common colour.
- Lighting is important. Spotlights create a more interesting effect than strip lights or ceiling bulbs alone.
- The dominant colour of your display also needs careful thought. Many colours have specific emotional associations.
- Props or accessories can be useful in displays. They should not be allowed to dominate a display, just to give it added interest.
- Few things lower a business's image more effectively than tatty price tickets. Unless you have very good handwriting, use Letraset or a proprietary ticketing machine.
- The outside of a business's premises are just as important as the interior. Point-of-sale material which can be used includes posters, billboards, standing signs, flags and bunting.
- Exterior signs and displays are controlled by local planning authorities through the Advertisement Regulations.
- Highway signs are a popular form of advertising for some businesses, especially those dependent on tourism and passing trade. Most such signs, in theory at least, require planning permission.
- Don't neglect to take advantage of the free advertising opportunities provided by your own transportation and on-site advertising boards.
- Exhibitions can provide an opportunity to meet several hundred potential buyers over the space of a few days, but attending can be expensive and time-consuming. Choose your exhibition carefully, and plan to ensure the success of your visit.
- Consider exhibiting at conferences, as these often include small exhibitions for the interest of delegates. Exhibiting in this way can be very cost-effective if you can find a conference aimed at people in your target market segment.
- Liaise with exhibition organisers over pre-exhibition

advertising. It may also be worth paying to advertise in the exhibition guide, but if you do so ensure that your advertisement gives people a compelling reason to visit your stand.

- Exhibition stands need to look interesting and welcoming. Displays help catch the eye, especially those which involve movement.
- Display boards need careful planning and design. Use large, colourful items, especially photos. Protect your boards from damage with a protective film or spray varnish.
- On the day, aim to look friendly and approachable, without coming across as overbearing. Concentrate on the serious prospects, and ensure you get their names, addresses and business titles.
- After the exhibition, follow up all enquiries promptly, evaluate the success (or otherwise) of your attendance, and see what lessons can be learned for the future.

CHAPTER NINE

SALES PROMOTIONS

The term 'sales promotion' covers a wide range of activities which are used to increase sales, generally in the short term. They are normally used in conjunction with press and other advertising. Although some types of sales promotion are mainly the province of large companies, others are easily adapted to the needs of smaller businesses.

Sales promotions cost money, adding to your overheads. However, they can still be profitable if they result in a significant increase in turnover. Their main use, however, is in attracting new customers who (you hope) will go on to become regulars even when the promotional period is over. For this reason, sales promotions are popular with businesses which depend on repeat custom, including many retailers, restaurants, mail order businesses, hotels and guest houses, entertainment and leisure operators, and a wide range of service businesses.

TYPES OF SALES PROMOTION
Sales promotions come in many different forms. Just a few possibilities include:

- Money-off vouchers.
- Competitions.
- Discounts.
- 'Sales'.
- Multi-packs (e.g. two-for-the-price-of-one).

- Banded offers (two different products sold together at a discount).
- Free gifts.
- Mail-ins.
- Free samples.
- Gift coupons.
- Loyalty schemes.

...and so on

The different methods will be examined in more detail later in the chapter.

'Advertising is the most fun you can have with your clothes on.'

Jerry Della Femina - American advertising executive

THE USES OF SALES PROMOTIONS

As mentioned above, sales promotions are used to give a (usually short-term) boost to sales. Some typical reasons for using a sales promotion include:

- To gain a foothold in the market when launching a new product.
- To help even out seasonal fluctuations in demand.
- To encourage more stockists to order the product.
- To raise public and dealer awareness.
- To gain free publicity (PR).

Every sales promotion should have a specific objective, measurable in terms of increased sales. If you run sales promotions just for the sake of it, the likelihood is you will be throwing money down the drain.

PRICE CUTTING

This is the commonest form of sales promotion. Used in conjunction with advertising ('Selected lines half price - one week only!'), it can be a highly effective way of attracting customers. Typical reasons for price cutting include:

1. With the launch of a new product, to penetrate the market quickly.
2. To defeat the launch of a rival's new product.
3. To generate more cash quickly - perhaps even to stay in business!
4. To clear out old stock before a new line is introduced.
5. As a loss leader, to draw people in to your premises and get them to buy other things as well.

6. To reach new customers in a market which has become saturated.
7. As a deliberate change in marketing strategy (perhaps aiming for a higher volume of sales with lower profit per item).
8. To improve the appearance of your balance sheet (cash reserves can look much better than a high stock figure).
9. To reduce the expense and inconvenience of stocktaking.
10. As a means of getting free publicity. For example, a pub might offer beer at 1940s prices for the first 100 customers.

Although popular, price cutting does have some drawbacks. Deciding how much to reduce prices by can be a problem. If you cut by too little, any effect will be marginal. On the other hand, if you cut prices by too much, people may regard your goods with suspicion ('They're much less than we usually pay. There must be something wrong with them!').

Price cutting also brings with it the risk of starting a price war. If you cut your prices, your rivals may cut theirs, and the only person who will end up benefiting is the consumer. In general, think hard about the possible consequences before you start a price cutting campaign. An alternative, if you can afford it, may be to relaunch your product with new packaging, a new form of promotion, and so on.

SALES

In sales, some or all of a business's products or services are sold at a lower price than was previously the case. According to the Trades Descriptions Act (1968), where goods are advertised at a reduced price, the higher price must have been charged for a continuous period of 28 days in the previous six months.

Sales can be an effective form of promotion, but if (as with certain nationally-advertised firms) you appear to have a year-round sale, the impact is inevitably reduced. As with all forms of sales promotion, a sale should aim to increase your normal, non-sale level of trading, by attracting new customers who then become regulars. Failing this, any short-term increase in business is likely to be offset by the costs involved.

MONEY-OFF VOUCHERS

Large companies frequently print money-off vouchers on their packaging in an attempt to build brand loyalty ('10p off your next purchase'). This principle can easily be adapted by smaller businesses. For example, you could include a coupon giving a discount on your product or service in your newspaper advertising or direct mail. This helps attract reader attention, and ensures that your advertising is read. Consumer research suggests that to be effective discounts should be worth 15% or more.

COMPETITIONS

Competitions can be a very effective way of raising interest in your product among the general public or retailers. Running a major competition can be a complex and time-consuming proposition, but again the idea can be adopted on a more modest scale by small businesses. A typical consumer competition consists of answering one or more questions related to the product, then completing a tie-breaker slogan ('I enjoy eating Crispy Snaps breakfast cereal because...')

The laws governing competitions are complex, and I recommend that you consult a solicitor if you are planning anything more ambitious than a small-scale local one. The main points to bear in mind are:

1. An element of skill must be present to distinguish the competition from a lottery.
2. Rules should be carefully worded and easy to understand.
3. The closing date must be clearly shown.
4. Proof of posting is not proof of delivery.
5. The number and sizes of prizes must be stated.
6. You must say if there are any restrictions, e.g. on who can enter, how many entries people can send, whether a proof of purchase is required, etc.

The British Code of Sales Promotion Practice includes detailed guidelines on running competitions. Copies are available from the Institute of Sales Promotion, the address of which is at the end of the chapter.

One idea some businesses might like to try is offering competition prizes for a local newspaper or special interest magazine. This can be a good way of generating extra interest in your product. For example, an artist known to the author offered a series of his prints to the local paper as competition prizes. As a result of the ensuing publicity, he obtained a number of valuable commissions. Similarly, the electronic publishers Way Ahead, mentioned elsewhere in this book, gave away a copy of their 'Creative Writing' tutorial as a competition prize for the magazine Writers' Monthly. They obtained valuable free publicity, and also received many sales leads in the form of the unsuccessful competition entrants.

MULTI-PACKS AND BANDED OFFERS

Typical multi-pack offers are 'Buy One, Get One Free' and 'Three For The Price Of Two'. In banded offers, by contrast, two different products are sold together at a discount price - for example, a can of paint may be sold with a 'free' brush. The aim of this type of offer is boost sales and, by making people buy more of your product, get them into the habit of using it.

CONTAINER PREMIUMS

This is a type of sales promotion which can be very effective for certain products. The container itself is seen as adding value to the product. For example, Cornish mead (a sweet wine made from honey) is sold in small pottery jars at a premium price. Other examples include luxury hampers which, when empty, make excellent picnic baskets; and beer shampoo sold in half-pint tankards which the purchaser can drink from when the shampoo is used up. I've also seen olive oil sold in containers made to resemble Greek amphoras. With a little imagination, containers can provide a valuable boost to a product's sales.

FREE GIFTS

Free gifts are a popular form of sales promotion. They can be used at the point of sale and in advertising as a means of attracting attention and securing extra orders; although - as with all sales promotions - the extra business must be set against the cost of the promotion itself. As ever, the main aim is to win new, regular customers. For example, many magazine publishers include a free gift for new subscribers, in the hope that, once people have been 'hooked', they will continue to subscribe in future.

One variation on the 'straight' free gift is the mail-in, where customers have to send away for the gift (perhaps with a set of tokens which they have collected). Care must be taken with this type of promotion that you have sufficient stocks of the gift to meet the response to your offer. In direct mail campaigns, free gifts are frequently used to ensure that the recipient replies quickly (e.g. 'Order within the next seven days and receive a mystery gift!').

Free gifts are used in a slightly different way as business incentives. They are given to regular customers to build or maintain goodwill, and also as a form of advertising. Perhaps the most popular type of business gift is the calendar: the hope is that this will find a place on your customer's wall, and remind him of your business every day of the year. Other gifts which can perform a similar function include diaries, engraved pens, wall clocks, maps, pocket calculators, mouse mats and so on. Various companies specialise in providing promotional gifts, and will print them for you with your business name and logo. One well-established company in this field is Healey Williams, Gift House,

94 Dedworth Road, Windsor, Berkshire, SL4 5AY (Tel: 01753 847847; Web: www.healeywilliams.co.uk).

CUSTOMER LOYALTY SCHEMES

These have been the marketing phenomenon of recent years. For example, all the major supermarket chains have taken advantage of new technology to launch loyalty card schemes. Typically, customers apply for a free, electronic 'smart card' from the store concerned. Every time they make a purchase at the store they present their card and points are added to it in proportion to the amount spent. These points are saved up, and can be exchanged for cash, discounts or free gifts.

As the name suggests, loyalty cards encourage customers to keep returning to the same store, the aim of any successful sales promotion. Stores can also obtain information from the cards about customers' individual spending patterns, and can use this to send targeted information about special offers etc. to those customers whose previous spending indicates that they might be most interested in them.

Small businesses may not have access to smart card technology, but they may be able to adapt this principle to their own circumstances. For example, a retailer might give all his customers during June a voucher entitling them to a 15% discount on all orders over £50 in July. Customer clubs and newsletters - further discussed in Chapter 12 - can help to encourage long-term customer loyalty.

THE INSTITUTE OF SALES PROMOTION

The Institute of Sales Promotion is a professional organisation of practitioners in this field. They are also concerned with setting and maintaining standards in sales promotion. They produce a range of useful leaflets and publications, including The British Code of Sales Promotion Practice (which includes detailed guidelines on running competitions). The address of the Institute of Sales Promotion is: Arena House, 66-68 Pentonville Road, London, N1 9HS (Tel: 020 7837 5340; Web: www.isp.org.uk). The Promotional Handling Association and the Sales Promotion Consultants' Association can also be contacted at this address.

KEY POINTS
- The term 'sales promotion' covers a wide range of activities which are used to increase sales in the short term.
- The reasons for using a sales promotion may include evening out seasonal fluctuations in demand, or gaining a foothold with a new product.
- Every sales promotion should have a specific objective,

measurable in terms of increased sales.

- Price cutting is the commonest form of sales promotion. It can be effective in generating extra turnover, but at the expense of profit.
- Sales are a form of across-the-board price cutting. One important aim is to attract new people into the shop, who will hopefully become regular customers.
- Money-off vouchers are a form of sales promotion which can easily be adapted by the small business. To be effective, discounts should be 15% or more.
- Competitions can be a good way of generating interest in your product, but can be complex and time-consuming to run. There are various legal requirements which must be adhered to.
- Selling products in unusual containers, or containers which have another use when empty, can be an effective way of boosting sales.
- Free gifts are another form of sales promotion. They can be used as a means of attracting attention and securing extra orders.
- Free gifts are often used in direct mail campaigns to encourage an immediate response.
- Free gifts can also be given out as business incentives. As well as generating goodwill, they serve as a form of advertising for your business.
- Customer loyalty schemes have been the marketing phenomenon of recent years. It is worth thinking whether you can adopt some such scheme for your own business.

CHAPTER TEN

RECRUITMENT ADVERTISING

Recruitment advertising differs in one important respect from the other advertising discussed in this book. Whereas the latter is aimed at attracting the attention of potential purchasers and persuading (or starting to persuade) them to buy, the main aim of recruitment advertising is to attract good quality applicants for vacancies you need to fill. A secondary aim is to deter people who do not have the qualities you require from applying, to avoid wasting their time and yours.

Although the aims are different, recruitment advertising requires at least as much thought and planning as advertising aimed at consumers. For one thing - and please forgive me for stating the obvious - a business is only as good as the people who work for it. No matter how skilled and dedicated you may be, if you are unable to attract high calibre staff the prospects for your business are limited. By contrast, a skilled and motivated workforce can multiply your business's productivity - and profitability - many times over.

A further reason why recruitment advertising is so important is that it projects an image of your business. Remember that it is not only potential job applicants who will see your ad, but customers and potential customers, your existing staff, and your competitors. The image you should be aiming to project is of a thriving, successful business which values its staff and treats them well.

Advertising which reflects poorly on your business, as well as being unlikely to attract good quality applicants, will lower the morale of your current employees, deter customers, and encourage the competition.

PREPARING A PERSON SPECIFICATION

Before you even think of sitting down to write your advertisement, it is important to spend some time thinking about the kind of person you require. It is a good idea to prepare a person specification. These show the qualifications, skills and experience you require for the job in question. You can sub-divide these into qualities that an applicant must have, and those which are merely desirable. For example, a simple person specification for a clerical assistant might appear as follows.

MUST HAVE	DESIRABLE
GCSE English	GCSE English grade A-C
	GCSE Commerce Business studies and/or Computer Science
Basic numeracy Typing skills Good telephone manner Neat handwriting	GCSE Mathematics Typing at 30 wpm Word processing experience Basic desktop publishing skills and experience
Commonsense and maturity	

Preparing a person specification will help you to visualise the person you require, an important preliminary to writing the advertisement. The person specification will also be available to send to enquirers so that they can see what qualities you are looking for and, if they believe themselves suitable, present their application accordingly.

> *'The true role of advertising is exactly that of the first salesman hired by the first manufacturer - to get business away from his competitors.'*

Rosser Reeves - American advertising executive

WRITING YOUR ADVERTISEMENT

What needs to go into a recruitment advertisement? As a bare minimum, I suggest the following:

- The title of the job.
- The name and address of the business.
- A telephone number, with contact name for enquiries.
- A clear description of the job.
- The wage or salary (including whether part or all is commission-based).
- Whether overtime is available and/or expected.
- Any specific requirements, e.g. experience or educational qualifications.

It is also worth mentioning if there are fringe benefits such as a staff canteen, luncheon vouchers, company pension scheme, private car park, etc., if only to show that yours is a company which cares about its employees. The same applies if you offer an above-average annual holiday entitlement or other benefits in kind.

Many advertisers do not quote specific salaries, preferring to leave this for negotiation with the person they appoint. However, if you state, 'Salary by arrangement' or some such, a number of potential candidates - including, perhaps, your ideal one - may be deterred through uncertainty from applying. You are also likely to receive applications from people who are over- or under-qualified. A possible compromise is to quote a salary range so that people can see the kind of money you anticipate paying, and so judge whether it would be worth their while applying.

Recruitment advertisements should be written in a concise, readable style. It is usually best to head the advertisement with the job title, as this is the first thing people scanning the ads will be looking for. Unless you are trying to attract 'creative' types, avoid the temptation to be witty. Set out the facts in a relaxed but informative way. Towards the end of the chapter you will find a number of sample recruitment ads which you can adapt for your own use.

AVOIDING DISCRIMINATION

When writing your ad, take care to avoid breaking the laws regarding race and sex discrimination. Small businesses must adhere to these as strictly as large. Thus, an advertisement for a 'Salesman' is likely to be seen as discriminatory. You could either amend this to 'Salesperson' or put in brackets after the job title 'male/female'. If you are in any doubt, the advertising department of the newspaper should be able to advise you.

Apart from breaking the law, advertisements which discriminate create a poor impression on many people who see them, and you may end up excluding someone who would be ideal for the job. Even if your ad does not discriminate directly, indirect discrimination can occur when, for instance, you specify that an applicant should come from a particular geographical area. This may be viewed as discrimination if the area in question is inhabited primarily by people from one particular ethnic group, especially if other neighbouring areas have a different ethnic composition.

Finally, there is - at the time of writing - no law against discrimination on the grounds of age. However, think twice before you put 'Age 20-24' (or whatever) in your advertisement. Such arbitrary limits eliminate at a stroke large numbers of older people who may be perfectly capable of performing the job you have in mind, and would perhaps bring to it additional maturity, loyalty and stability.

WHERE (AND HOW) TO ADVERTISE

For most small businesses, the obvious starting point will be the local paper, and this is generally fine for unskilled and semi-skilled jobs where you hope to appoint someone living locally. Many areas are covered by two or more local papers, but there is usually one which contains substantially more job ads than the others. This will be the paper job seekers make a point of reading, and is likely to be the best place to advertise your own vacancy.

Local papers published daily often have one particular day of the week on which most job ads appear, and again this is the best day to place your own advertisement. The Birmingham Evening Mail, for example, includes by far the greatest number of job ads on a Thursday, and many job seekers buy the paper on this day if no other.

For many vacancies, especially unskilled and semi-skilled, a classified advertisement should be sufficient. Local papers usually run such ads under a number of headings, e.g. Sales, Clerical, Industrial, Hair and Beauty, Driving, Computers, Secretarial, Part-time, and so on. People seeking a job automatically look under the heading they are most interested in.

Display advertising is more eye-catching than classified, of course, but it is also much more expensive. It is used mainly for better-paid professional and managerial jobs, where advertisers wish to attract the attention of people who are likely to be in work already and may not even be looking for another job at the moment. If you want your ad to stand out without spending a fortune on display advertising, a semi-display ad in the classified section may be a suitable compromise.

For more specialised and senior posts, local papers may not offer adequate coverage. One possibility is to advertise in national newspapers. Different papers specialise in different fields. For example, the Daily Telegraph has traditionally been the place to look for sales representatives' jobs, while the Monday Guardian is where the majority of creative and media vacancies are advertised. Advertising in national newspapers is expensive, of course, and another option worth considering is advertising in the relevant trade and professional journals. For example, a vacancy for a civil engineer could be advertised in Construction Weekly, a vacancy for a farm manager in Farmers' Weekly or Farming News.

SAMPLE ADVERTISEMENTS
The sample advertisements below are based on actual advertisements used in local newspapers. They illustrate a range of possible approaches, and can be adapted as required for your own advertising.

RETAIL MANAGER
Must have a minimum of three years' retail experience, preferably with management responsibilities. An ideal opportunity to join a young and expanding company with a chain of pet superstores. Salary £00000 with excellent prospects. Send application in writing with CV to: ....

WATSON's FINANCIAL SERVICES LIMITED
require INDEPENDENT FINANCIAL ADVISORS

- Candidates must be FPC qualified.
- Minimum three years' experience Tied/IFA.
- Superb self-employed package.
- East Midlands based company founded 1963.
- Large client bank and regular new leads.
- Full marketing support.

Enquiries to Tracey Cunliffe on ....

TECHNICAL SUPPORT OFFICER

Exciting opportunity for experienced technicians to join a dynamic office-based support team. The ideal candidate will be qualified to MCP standard or equivalent. However, relevant technical support experience of at least two years would be considered. Must be organised, presentable and possess a good telephone manner.
Salary up to £00000 p.a. dependent on experience.
If you are enthusiastic about developing a career in technical support, send your CV by post to Peter Woodmansey, ...

EXPERIENCED TOOLMAKER

A & G Manufacturing Limited require an all-round precision toolmaker with an engineering background. The successful applicant must have experience of progression tooling for small components and be able to follow through to try-out stage.

In return for total commitment and flexibility to accommodate peak periods, we offer excellent career prospects and a competitive salary working within a good clean environment. Please apply in writing enclosing full CV and detailing current/expected salary to: Personnel Office, ...

STOREKEEPER/DRIVER

£00000 - £00000 p.a.

Required to undertake various basic stores duties and provide a messenger delivery service between the company's various sites. You should be a qualified operator of an electric reach truck, possess a clean current driving licence, have had experience in a modern stores, and be competent in English and Mathematics. A good geographical knowledge of the local area is required.

For an application form and further particulars returnable by .... send a postcard quoting job reference number .... and your name and address to: The Personnel Officer, ...

KEY POINTS

- The key aim of recruitment advertising is to attract suitable applicants for positions you need to fill. A secondary aim is to deter unsuitable candidates from applying.
- Recruitment advertising requires at least as much thought and planning as advertising aimed at consumers. Recruiting high calibre staff is crucial to a business's continuing success and expansion.
- Recruitment advertising also projects an image of your business to other people - not only potential job applicants, but customers, competitors and existing staff. It is therefore important your advertising projects a positive image.
- Before writing your ad, spend some time preparing a person specification. This will help you visualise the kind of applicant you hope to attract. You can then write the ad accordingly.

- Ensure that your ad includes all the basic facts about the job. If you offer fringe benefits such as a staff canteen or pension scheme, it may be worth mentioning these as well.
- Try to give specific information about wages or salary levels. If you do not wish to commit yourself, consider quoting a range.
- Write your ad in a concise, readable style. Unless aiming to attract 'creative' types, avoid the temptation to be witty.
- Avoid discriminating on grounds of sex or race in your advertisement. Not only is it against the law, it will also create a poor impression with many readers.
- If you plan to specify that applicants should come from within a certain area, be aware of the possibility that you may be accused of indirect discrimination.
- Age discrimination is not (yet) illegal, but think carefully before specifying age limits. For many positions, older people can perform at least as good a job as younger ones.
- For unskilled and semi-skilled jobs, an ad in your local paper should attract sufficient applicants.
- Choose the local paper which includes most recruitment advertising, and advertise on the day of the week when most such ads appear.
- For many jobs, especially unskilled and semi-skilled, a classified ad under the appropriate heading should be adequate.
- If you want to attract the attention of casual browsers as well as active job seekers, you may need to consider display advertising. To keep costs down, a semi-display ad is a possible compromise.
- For skilled technical and professional staff, you may need to advertise more widely. National newspapers are one possibility, and you could also try advertising in the relevant trade or professional journals.

CHAPTER ELEVEN

PUBLIC RELATIONS

Some would argue that public relations - commonly known as PR - has no place in a book about advertising. This is because PR does not attempt to sell directly. Rather, it aims to create goodwill and understanding for the business concerned and its products/services. Advertising and salesmanship then convert this into actual sales.

Viewed in this light, PR might seem a luxury for the small business. That is far from being the case. One reason is that, like it or not, every business has to have public relations, if you define this simply as 'relations with the public'. Relations may be good, bad or indifferent, but if your business has a poor reputation then no amount of expensive advertising will overcome it. Conversely, if you have a good reputation, word of mouth alone may bring in a steady stream of new customers, with advertising just 'the icing on the cake'.

Public relations is really all about being aware of your business's reputation, and doing everything you can to protect and improve it. Effective PR creates goodwill, and ensures that your advertising and other forms of promotion are effective. In addition, PR can provide valuable, low cost advertising in its own right. Before looking at specific PR techniques for small businesses, however, we need to spend a few moments looking at how and why PR works.

DEFINITION

I have already suggested one, rather simplistic, definition of public relations: relations with the public. A more scientific definition is offered by the (British) Institute of Public Relations (IPR). Their definition is as follows:

'Public relations practice is the planned and sustained effort to establish and maintain goodwill and mutual understanding between an organisation and its publics.'

The IPR definition underlines the point that public relations is not about selling, but creating goodwill and understanding. Other aspects of the definition may require a few words of explanation.

PUBLICS

In PR-speak, the word 'public' is used in a rather different sense from the usual one ('the general public'). A business's publics are the various groups with which it must communicate. A typical organisation has up to a dozen different publics. In the case of a small to medium-sized business, these might include:

1. Customers.
2. Potential customers.
3. Employees.
4. Potential employees.
5. The local community.
6. Suppliers.
7. Distributors.
8. The money market.
9. Local opinion leaders.

Each of these groups has a different interest and role in the business, and must be communicated with in a different way. It follows that public relations addresses a larger and more varied audience than the target market segments addressed in advertising. Although this book is mainly concerned with the role of PR in advertising, it is worth bearing in mind that good PR is important across every aspect of a business's operations.

PLANNING AND OBJECTIVES

Another point made in the IPR definition is that PR is a 'planned and sustained effort'. Public relations needs to be planned on a long-term basis; it is not something which happens overnight. If you are launching a new and innovative product, for example, you may need to prepare an extensive PR programme, including press releases, articles, press conferences, and so on.

All PR should have clearly defined objectives (things you hope to achieve). This involves identifying who are your target publics, and tailoring your PR strategy to reach them. As far as possible, objectives should be defined in measurable terms. One method of measurement is the amount of media coverage obtained (usually measured by the column inch). A successful PR campaign may achieve the equivalent of many thousands of pounds of paid-for advertising.

USING THE MEDIA

You may have noticed that one item not included in our list of a business's publics was 'the media' (newspapers, radio and TV, etc.). That is because the media represent the channels through which a business's publics are communicated with, rather than being the publics themselves (though some journalists may be included in the category of local opinion leaders, in which case they become a 'public' in their own right).

In order to communicate with their publics, businesses must use a range of media. To communicate with staff a noticeboard or newsletter may be sufficient, but reaching other groups such as potential customers requires the use of external media. These may include local and national newspapers, the trade press, TV and radio, and so on.

With advertising you buy space in the media of your choice and can - within reason and the law - say anything you like. PR operates rather differently. For one thing, your aim in PR is to inform and educate rather than to persuade. You could, of course, buy space in a publication then use it for PR announcements, and indeed businesses do sometimes do this (e.g. when a faulty product has to be recalled). However, this has the disadvantage that it will cost just as much as an advertisement - and, in addition, people will see that the coverage has been paid for by the business, and may therefore be inclined to take whatever it says with the proverbial pinch of salt.

For small businesses in particular, much PR activity involves attempting to gain free coverage in the news and feature pages of the relevant media. Editors are always looking for material to fill their pages, and if you have a good story which they think would interest their readers, there is every chance that they will run it. PR involves bringing such stories to editors' attention, and making it as easy as possible for them to find out more. The great advantage of obtaining coverage in this way is that the information will appear as a news or feature item rather than an advertisement. Readers are therefore more likely to see the information as truthful and unbiased.

DO YOU NEED A PR AGENCY?

It is possible to engage an outside agency to handle aspects of public relations, but for many small businesses this may be neither necessary nor desirable. While advertising agencies are able to offset some of their fees from commission they receive on advertisements booked, PR agencies have to charge the going rate for all their work. Few agencies are interested in taking on a new client unless they anticipate a fee income of £1,000 a month or more from them.

Fortunately, it is perfectly possible for most small businesses to handle their own PR. Indeed, when dealing with media enquiries on matters such as new products, the business itself is likely to be better placed to provide answers than any agency.

As your business grows, however, you may find occasions arising when engaging a PR agency may be worthwhile. These could include:

- A major new product launch.
- A business take-over or expansion.
- A significant new discovery or innovation.
- A major accident or other misfortune affecting the public.

In these circumstances, a PR agency may be able to supplement your own efforts, ensuring that you gain maximum benefit from the news value of your story, or (in the latter case) minimising any bad publicity.

PRESS RELEASES

I mentioned earlier that much PR in small businesses involves attempting to gain 'free' editorial coverage in newspapers and other media. By far the commonest way of doing this is by means of a press release. A press release is a short article which you hope will be published by the newspaper or magazine concerned, or prompt one of their reporters to write a piece based on it.

Press releases must concern something newsworthy, as papers will not simply print a piece saying how wonderful your business is. Nevertheless, trade magazines and local newspapers in particular are often under-staffed and welcome good stories they can use, even if the news they contain is not particularly earth-shattering. Some events which would certainly justify a press release include:

- The opening of your business.
- The launch of a new product or service.
- Winning a big order.
- Export success.

- Winning a prize or award.
- Celebrating an anniversary.
- Appointing a new manager.
- Moving to larger premises.
- Installation of new plant or technology.
- Good financial results.
- Success of trainees or apprentices.
- Involvement with charities or other good works.

WRITING YOUR PRESS RELEASE

A press release should NOT be written in the same way as an advertisement. The idea is to achieve coverage in the editorial pages, so you should try to imitate the style used for features and news stories in your target publication/s. This will usually be balanced, concise and factual, avoiding the 'hyped' tones of an advertisement.

Your aim in writing a press release should be to produce a story which could be used by the editor without requiring any changes. If your release is published more or less as you wrote it, you can congratulate yourself on a job well done! The main principles of press release writing are summarised below.

1. All press releases should be typed or word processed. Type on only one side of the paper, and use double spacing (alternate 'empty' lines). Leave at least one-inch left- and right-hand margins, and indent the first line of every new paragraph except the first by five characters.
2. Under your letterhead type the date and the heading PRESS RELEASE in block capitals. If you do not wish your story to be printed until a certain date you can write EMBARGO: 1 JULY 2000 (or whatever), but do not do this unless you have a very good reason. Newspapers do not like embargoes, although they will usually respect them.
3. Below this, write a heading for the release. This should explain in a nutshell what the release is about - for example NEW RESTAURANT OPENS IN BRIGHTSEA or STAR MOTORS WINS NATIONAL AWARD. The heading should be centred and written in block capitals.
4. Below this, write the text of your press release. As already mentioned, this should be in news story rather than advertisement style. Aim to answer as concisely as possible the five Ws - WHO, WHAT, WHEN, WHERE and WHY. That is to say, WHO you are, WHAT you have done, WHEN you did it, WHERE you did it, and WHY you did it. Try to cover all the main points in the first couple of paragraphs, as the lower half of the release may be cut if the editor is short of

space. If at all possible, keep your press release to a single page. If you have to go on to a second page, write at the bottom of the first page 'more follows' and at the start of the next 'continued'. No press release should be longer than two pages.

5. If possible, include a quote from yourself or someone else in your business. This can lighten the tone of the release and make it look more like a 'proper' news story. If you want to include matters of opinion in a press release, they should always be put in quotations (e.g. 'We are now the best-known widget-making company in Europe,' said Managing Director Bill Smith). Matters of fact, as opposed to opinion, can be given straight without the need for quotes.

6. It will help if you can include a photograph to accompany the release. Sharp, glossy prints with good contrast are preferred. Avoid dull mug-shots and formal group pictures - if at all possible, show something interesting and unusual taking place. Alternatively, if the occasion merits it, you could include a note at the end of your release that photographers will be welcome at the presentation at 12.30 p.m., or whatever is appropriate.

7. At the end of the release, include a phone number where a reporter can contact you to get more information.

WHERE TO SEND YOUR RELEASE

The publications to which you should send your press release depend on the target publics you wish to reach. The main choices are as follows:

Trade press

These publications are generally receptive to press releases concerning their area of interest. Research has shown that 40% of buying decisions in large firms are based on information from trade and technical magazines - so if you hope to sell to such businesses, it is important to feed the trade press with regular press releases.

Consumer magazines

These are bought by members of the public rather than businesses. Again, they are generally receptive to press releases concerning their area of interest. A press release concerning a company's new range of fishing tackle, for example, would be well worth sending to angling magazines. This can be a good way of reaching consumers with an interest in your particular product or service. It may be most effective when combined with advertising in the magazine concerned.

Below is an example of a press release to give you an idea of what they look like.

PRESS RELEASE

July 3 2000

NEW THAI RESTAURANT OPENS IN LITTLETOWN

A new restaurant serving Thai cuisine, The Summer Palace, opens on Saturday 8 July in Bridge Street, Littletown. The Summer Palace is named after the ancient and beautiful building of that name in Thailand's capital, Bangkok.

Among the attractions on the menu will be 'steamboat'. This is a traditional Thai dish, where diners cook strips of meat, fish and vegetables in stock on a small burner in the middle of the table, and eat them with rice and noodles.

The proprietor of The Summer Palace, Anne Sereywath, says: 'At present the choice of places to eat out in Littletown is limited to Indian and Chinese. We aim to give people here a wider choice and introduce them to some new foods, and new ways of eating them!'

As a special opening offer, every diner at The Summer Palace during the first week will be given a complimentary glass of red or white wine. Bookings are now being taken on 01302 787543.

Further information: Anne Sereywath Tel: 01302 787543 (day/evening)

Local press

Local newspapers are always keen to receive 'good news' stories concerning businesses in their area. Information concerning new appointments, awards, anniversaries, celebrations and export successes is well worth passing on. Local papers are read by most people in the area they cover, so sending them regular press releases can be good way of ensuring that, locally, your business remains in the public eye.

Regional press

As with local papers, regional newspapers and magazines are always interested to receive press releases about businesses in their area, but the news they contain needs to be a little more substantial. A major export order from Russia would stand a fair chance of inclusion, a move to new premises less so.

National press

These are likely to be a poor bet for stories concerning technical developments, new appointments, anniversaries, moves, and so on. On the other hand, if you have a good human interest story they may be worth trying. The tabloid press, in particular, often picks up on quirky stories about people and businesses doing unusual things.

Broadcast media

It may also be worth sending your press release to local, regional or national TV and radio companies. This is discussed in more detail later in this chapter.

You can send your press release to the editor, or to the reporter who covers small business matters for the publication. The chances are that you will already be aware of the publications which cover your area of business, but if not there is a number of media guides you can consult. They are expensive to buy, but are available in larger public libraries. They include:

- Benn's Press Directory.
- Hollis Press and Public Relations Annual.
- PIMS Media Directory.
- PR Planner UK.
- PR Planner Europe.
- Willings Press Guide.

Don't expect to succeed every time you send out a press release - yours may be competing with hundreds of others - but when you do manage to get coverage the amount of interest it generates can more than justify the effort you put in. If you find you enjoy writing press releases and have some success with them, you could try your hand at writing short articles, perhaps for trade or technical magazines. You should not expect to be paid for such articles, but will benefit from the publicity they generate.

> *'On the average, five times as many people read the headlines as read the body copy. It follows that unless your headline sells your product, you have wasted 90 per cent of your money.'*

David Ogilvy - British advertising executive

PRESS CONFERENCES

Most of the time press releases will serve your PR needs quite adequately, but once in a while you may find yourself with a major story which press releases alone will not do justice to. This is the time to consider holding a press conference.

Holding a press conference is not a decision to be taken lightly. It will require careful planning, and is likely to involve no small expense. A press conference is a high-risk activity - your business will be firmly in the media spotlight, and if for some reason the event goes badly it will reflect unfavourably on the business itself. The time to hold a press conference is when you have some dramatic and exciting news to impart. Naturally, what counts as dramatic and exciting depends very much on the media sector you have targeted. Possible examples would include:

- The launch of a new and innovative product.
- The announcement of a major award, e.g. The Queen's Award for Exports.
- A large-scale sponsorship or charitable initiative.
- A business take-over or expansion.
- A new training or employment opportunity.

A press conference should NOT be held if there is any doubt as to its success. Neither should you hold one if there is no really newsworthy information to pass on. If there is any doubt in your mind as to whether to hold a press conference, it may be better just to issue a press release instead.

CHOOSING A VENUE

Choosing the right venue is very important. On any day you are likely to be competing with several hundred other press conferences. The venue can be a major influence on how many journalists turn up.

It can be a good idea to choose an unusual setting, either in contrast with your message or to reinforce it. Finding a place that hasn't been used before will give your conference novelty value to make it stand out from the rest.

In general, avoid using your own premises (unless the event is to mark the opening of a new factory, etc.). Choose somewhere reasonably easy to find with good access and parking. If the place you choose is difficult to get to, lay on transport from some central point.

Finally, if your aim is to attract the national media, the venue will have to be in London. Their journalists do not have the time - or perhaps the inclination - to leave the capital.

WHEN TO HOLD YOUR PRESS CONFERENCE

No one day is automatically better than any other, but try to avoid clashing with other major events, especially those which you know will tie up journalists who might otherwise attend your press conference.

The time also merits careful thought. Despite their popular image, most journalists are busy people and prefer to avoid long, boozy lunch time events. A good time of day is mid-morning (somewhere between 10 and 11 a.m.), with the provision of coffee and light refreshments only. If this is stated on the invitation, journalists know that they will be able to attend your conference, stay for half an hour or so, then go on to their next appointment.

SENDING INVITATIONS

Send out invitations, if possible to named journalists, at least a few days in advance. Your invitation can take various forms:

- A press release with invitation attached.
- A formal printed card (usually used when a major ceremony is involved).
- A letter.
- A gimmick (e.g. a publishing company might send its invitation in the form of a dummy book).

Avoid giving away too much in your invitation - your aim is to whet the journalists' appetites, but not to tell them so much that they don't have to come to your press conference. Enclose a map of the venue, with notes on the best routes to get there. State on the invitation if and when there will be a photo-call (an opportunity to take photographs).

Phone around shortly before the event to see how many of the people you invited are actually coming (you can always make the excuse that you need to know for catering purposes). However, don't expect all those who say they will attend to actually turn up on the day.

AT THE CONFERENCE

Ensure that you and any of your staff who are attending are well presented and well briefed. In particular, warn your staff against making off-the-cuff comments which they (and you) will regret later. It is important to agree on the line you will take beforehand, and then stick to it.

It can also be a good idea to prepare a press pack. This is a pack of information you can give out to those who attend, and post off to those who don't. Your press pack should consist of a printed folder containing as a minimum:

- A press release giving full details of what the event is about.
- Background information on the company/product.
- Photographs of people quoted in the press release.

It is customary to begin the conference with a brief, not-too-technical presentation. This may consist of one or two speeches and, if appropriate, a demonstration. After this, you can invite questions from the assembled journalists. It is probably best not to give out press packs until the end, or you will be competing with the packs for the journalists' attention.

At the end of the conference, ask the photographers attending for any spare pictures for your files. Some of the photos they take are certain not to be used, and they will probably let you have them inexpensively. The pictures may be useful for your own future publicity.

Finally, as mentioned, send those who did not attend a press pack in the post. There is even a case for sending a spare pack to those who DID attend, as packs are sometimes mislaid between the press conference and the newspaper office.

TV AND RADIO

With TV and radio stations proliferating, there are increasing opportunities for small businessmen to gain valuable publicity. You can obtain TV coverage in just the same way as with printed media, by sending a press release to the newsroom of the TV station in question. The early evening regional programmes (e.g. Midlands Today, Look North) are often the most receptive to items about local businesses. Send your press release to arrive at the TV station in good time. The best type of story to offer includes:

- Good news
- Human interest
- Visual appeal (something interesting to show on the TV screen)
- And is in some way quirky or unusual

Even more so than newspaper offices, TV newsrooms are in a state of perpetual chaos, with priorities changing all the time as fresh news stories break (or fail to). Often you will hear nothing for days, then receive a phone call a few hours before the programme is due to go out asking you to make arrangements for a film crew to arrive, or to drop everything and come into the studio This is how TV works, and there is not much you can do except be prepared for this and try to keep your diary free.

APPEARING ON TELEVISION

The first time you appear on television can be a daunting experience, but on successive occasions it will become more enjoyable. Following the points opposite should help to make your first time relatively painless.

1. Check with the researcher or programme assistant (whoever contacts you to arrange the interview) what 'angle' they are adopting. Is it just a local good news story, or does the producer have some other agenda? If you have been invited to a studio discussion, find out who the other guests will be. If they are likely to be hostile to you or your business, you will need to be well-briefed.
2. Find out whether the programme will be live or recorded. Live programmes have more bite and impact, and the additional advantage that the programme-maker cannot edit what you say. On the other hand, with live programmes you only have one chance. With a recorded programme, if you make a hash of things, you can always say, 'I'm sorry, could we do that bit again, please?'
3. Once you know the format of the programme, you can start to plan your approach. Fix on two or three key points which you want to get over. One thing you must avoid is going into the studio with only a vague, general notion of what you want to say.

ON THE DAY

1. Arrive at the TV studio in good time. Wear reasonably sober colours, avoiding too many checks and lines as these can affect the picture. Studios can be hot, airless places, so ensure that your clothing is light and comfortable.
2. Avoid alcoholic drinks beforehand, even to settle your nerves; at the interview you will need all your wits about you. Be sure you are comfortable (i.e. you have visited the toilet!) before the interview starts.
3. If possible, have a word with the interviewer to try to find out what questions he plans to ask. He should be willing to give

you a general idea, though, in the interests of spontaneity, he is unlikely to give you chapter and verse.

4. At the interview, sit forward in your seat, leaning slightly forward. This will help you look (and feel) alert. Through the interview look at the interviewer, not the camera.
5. Speak clearly and distinctly. Many people when they are nervous tend to gabble. If you know this applies to you, make a conscious effort to slow down.
6. There is no need to sit on your hands during an interview, but avoid excessive gestures and mannerisms, as they will distract and irritate the viewer. Avoid smoking during the interview, as this can give you a seedy image.
7. Your aim should be to come across as sincere and enthusiastic. Remember that you are appearing in many thousands - perhaps millions - of viewers' homes. Try to appear relaxed and friendly. Above all, remember to SMILE!
8. Memorise your two or three prepared points, and ensure that you make these no matter what. If the interviewer appears to be missing the point, there are various ways of bringing his questions round your way. For example:

- *'You must remember that...'*
- *'I'll come to that in a moment, but first...'*
- *'What I would really like to say is...'*
- *'That's an interesting point, but don't you think that..?'*
- *'The fact of the matter is...'*

DEALING WITH AWKWARD INTERVIEWS

Most of the time interviews should be relaxed and enjoyable, but once in a while you may come up against an abrasive interviewer who is determined to put you and your business on the spot. In these circumstances, it is essential to be well prepared.

1. If the interviewer rephrases your statements, make sure he gets them right, and correct them at once if not. Similarly, refute immediately any incorrect statements.
2. If possible, keep back some information in support of your case: a new report, latest government statistics, etc. If necessary you can then produce this in the interview, and hopefully stop the interviewer in his tracks.
3. Another good tactic is to give a short answer then stop. The interviewer will be hoping you will put your foot in it, but if you remain silent he will have to ask something else. Never feel obliged to say something to fill a silence: this is the interviewer's job.
4. If you are being prevented from making your point, carry on

talking, even over the interviewer. He will normally let you continue, as two people talking at once makes bad television.

5. Try to remain calm and courteous, even if you feel you are being provoked. Avoid, above all, losing your temper. In the eyes of the TV audience you will then come across as the person who has been wronged, thus generating a sympathetic audience reaction.

6. Finally, answer a trick question with another question:

- *'Do you really believe that?'*
- *'Why don't you ask..?'*

APPEARING ON RADIO

Many of the principles above also apply with radio. As there are many more radio stations than TV, your chances of success with radio are actually much better. Local radio stations, in particular, are constantly looking for good news stories in their area, and if you feed them with regular press releases there is every chance that some of them will result in coverage. You will also find yourself being phoned up by stations seeking your comments about matters relevant to your business. This can be an excellent way of keeping yourself and your business in the public eye locally.

HANDLING THE TELEPHONE INTERVIEW

A popular method of recording radio interviews is over the phone. A word of caution is in order, however. Don't be tempted to reply off-the-cuff when a radio reporter phones you up. Ask him what questions he wants to ask, then say you will phone him back in a few minutes. This will give you a chance to decide on the main points you wish to make, and ensure you have all the necessary information at your fingertips.

Before you phone back, move into a quieter room. Take any other phones off the hook and stop any computer printers or photocopiers. Have any information you will require (e.g. telephone numbers to give out) in front of you. While the interview is going on, avoid tapping your pen or shuffling your papers.

RADIO TECHNIQUES

Whether you are interviewed over the phone or in a recording studio, there are certain techniques you can learn. Many of these are the same as those listed under television. Above all, in radio you must speak clearly and distinctly, avoiding any temptation to rush or gabble. Some further tips are:

- Avoid hesitations or long pauses, as they will make you sound evasive.
- Avoid speaking in a monotone - vary the pace and emphasis of your speech.
- Aim to sound bright and enthusiastic.
- Even though listeners will not see it, try to smile while you are speaking. Listeners will hear the good-humour in your voice.
- Avoid giving 'yes' or 'no' answers. Every question is an opportunity which you should use to get your point across.

PHONE-IN PROGRAMMES

These have become increasingly popular as a means of involving a radio station's listeners and filling air-time cheaply. For the businessman who can think on his feet, they can provide a marvellous PR opportunity. If you are invited to appear on a phone-in programme, it is an opportunity which you should accept with alacrity.

One hint is to take along a few standard reference books on your subject in case you are asked something you are hazy about. It is better to admit that you don't know an answer than to make one up.

Finally, bear in mind that TV and radio stations pay appearance fees, but may forget unless you ask. Naturally, TV pays better.

OTHER PR METHODS

In addition to those already mentioned, there is a wide range of other methods for generating goodwill and publicity. These include:

'There are a million definitions of public relations. I have found it to be the craft of arranging the truth so that people will like you.'

Alan Harrington - American writer

Sponsorship

The FA Carling Premiership, the Nationwide League and the Guinness Book of Records are all examples of large-scale sponsorship. They are effective and relatively painless ways of generating favourable publicity for the companies concerned.

There is no reason why smaller businesses could not adopt a similar approach in their local area. For example, you could offer to sponsor the local cricket or football team, in exchange for publicity at the ground and in match programmes. You could even offer to provide the team kit (with your company logo, of course, tastefully embroidered on the front!).

Sponsorship need not only be sporting, of course. You could equally offer to sponsor the local theatre or opera company - this could be an effective way to get your name noticed by their predominantly middle-class audience. Even small-scale sponsorship, such as the loan of a company vehicle to take part in the town carnival, can help build goodwill locally. Another possibility is to sponsor a local competition or award.

Charitable support

There are many ways in which businesses can support charities and other good causes without spending vast amounts. They include:

- Donations - cash gifts to registered charities are usually tax deductible, although check first with your accountant.
- Providing expertise - perhaps you could offer your skills (e.g. computers, law, accounting) to a charity which needs them. You could also offer to sit on their management committee.
- Providing rooms and facilities - for example, one company allows a local charity to use its board room for their management committee meetings. Another provides use of the company mini-bus and driver to take elderly people from a local day centre on outings.
- Donating spare or obsolete supplies and equipment - even though your old 386 computer is no longer at the cutting edge of technology, it may be just the thing a local charity needs for its word processing and mailing lists.
- Employee volunteering - here you offer the services of your staff, perhaps one day a month or half a day a week, to assist a local charity. The Body Shop, for example, allows its staff to participate in this if they wish. As well as the goodwill generated, they find it valuable as a means of management training and development.
- Use of design, desktop publishing and printing facilities - many charities have to operate on a shoestring, and design and printing is one of their major expenses. If you have facilities which you can offer - perhaps at nominal cost - it will be greatly appreciated.
- Publicise the charities' activities and needs on your company noticeboard or in your staff newsletter.

If you wish to support local charities but are not sure where to start, the best place to contact is your local Council for Voluntary Service (CVS). CVSs represent and serve local charities, and will put you in touch with organisations who are interested in what you have to offer. The address should be in the phone book, or contact the National Association of Councils for Voluntary Service (NACVS), 177 Arundel Court, Arundel Street, Sheffield, S1 2NU (tel. 0114 278 6636).

Open days
Another option is to hold an open day. Invite your staff and their partners, suppliers, customers and prospects, neighbouring businesses, local dignitaries and the media. Provide a light buffet and some liquid refreshment. Have something interesting going on for people to see, and put up displays and photographs. Prepare some interesting and entertaining speeches and demonstrations. An open day can be a very effective way of generating goodwill and publicity.

Newsletters
A newsletter for customers and prospects can be a very worthwhile PR investment. This is especially so for service businesses, where you can use it to show the variety of clients you have worked with and projects you have completed. Send out your newsletter every three months or so. It will provide a gentle reminder of the range of services you have to offer, and is very likely to result in enquiries and sales.

Public speaking
Accept any invitation you receive to speak in public on your field of expertise, and circulate local groups with information about your availability. Many groups regularly invite guest speakers to talk about their specialist subjects - just a few examples include Lions Clubs, Women's Institutes, Rotary Clubs, Chambers of Commerce, Junior Chambers, and so on.

Public speaking does not come naturally to everyone, but most people's skills do improve with practice. The following pointers may help:

- Find out as much as possible beforehand about your audience. You need to know whether they are expecting to be informed or entertained, what assumptions you can make about their level of knowledge, and so on.
- Choose a topic which is appropriate to the setting and your audience. It is best to structure your speech around a single theme or objective.
- Take time to prepare your speech well. Research any facts and other information you will use.
- Practise your speech a few times beforehand in private.
- Avoid simply reading from notes, as this will come over as flat and dull.

- Have a note of the main points you want to make, key phrases, and any facts and figures you wish to quote.
- Speak clearly and distinctly, avoiding any temptation to gabble.
- Vary your pace and tone. Emphasise key points with a pause, by lowering your voice, and by movement and gesture.
- A touch of humour always goes down well, especially any amusing anecdotes related to your business.
- Visual aids such as slides or a video can be very helpful, though ensure that any equipment you need will be available at the venue (or take your own).
- If you can incorporate some kind of demonstration into your talk, do.

Public speaking engagements should not be seen as selling opportunities, but you never know who might be in the audience and what it might lead to. Be sure to leave some leaflets or business cards in a prominent place for anyone who might want to contact you subsequently.

How-to-do-it guides
This is another highly effective PR device. For example, a dry cleaning firm might produce a guide on how to remove difficult stains, a removal firm a leaflet on everything you need to consider when moving home. These can be sent or given to customers and prospects, and immediately create goodwill towards the company concerned. In addition, an informative leaflet may be kept for future reference; and every time the recipient sees it, they will be subtly reminded of your business.

Other ideas
PR is one area where you can allow your imagination free rein. Some other ideas which you could use or adapt include:

- A local Indian restaurant gives out a free red carnation to every lady customer as she is leaving.
- A butcher keeps a jar of sweets under his counter, and gives one to every child who comes in (so children always want to drag their parents into the shop).
- A restaurant asks when any children in a group have birthdays. They then send out a card and free meal invitation to the child just before (of course, the parents have to come too...)
- After a service, a garage leaves a paper tissue in the car with the message, 'The steering wheel and controls have been cleaned by our mechanic, but the tissue is for your added convenience'.
- Another garage sends customers a 'birthday card' on the anniversary of purchasing their car, reminding them of their continued interest.

As with all PR, in no case is there any direct attempt to sell anything; but by creating goodwill and understanding, the businesses create a climate in which enquiries and sales are much more likely to result.

KEY POINTS

- Public relations does not attempt to sell directly. Rather, it aims to create goodwill and understanding for the business concerned.
- PR has been defined by the Institute of Public Relations as, '...the planned and sustained effort to establish and maintain goodwill and mutual understanding between an organisation and its publics.'
- A business's publics are the various groups with which it must communicate: staff, customers, suppliers, etc.
- Public relations needs to be planned and implemented over a period – it is not something that happens overnight. All PR activity should have clearly defined, measurable objectives.
- For small businesses, much PR activity involves attempting to gain free coverage in the editorial pages of the relevant media..
- The great advantages of PR coverage are that it is free, and people are more likely to see the news it contains as truthful and unbiased.
- Most small businesses are capable of handling their own PR. As a business grows, however, there may be occasions when engaging a PR agency could be desirable.
- The usual way of feeding stories to the media is via a press release. This is a short article which you hope will be published by a newspaper or magazine, or prompt a reporter to write a piece based on it.
- A press release should be written in the factual, objective style of a news report. It is important that it concerns something newsworthy.
- A press release should answer the five Ws - Who, What, Where, When and Why - as concisely as possible.
- A press release should normally include one or two quotes. Quotes should always be used when you wish to convey information based on opinion rather than fact.
- The main choices of media to send press releases are the trade press, consumer magazines, local newspapers, regional newspapers, national newspapers, TV and radio.
- To find out the media serving your area of interest, you can consult guides such as Hollis and PR Planner UK.
- When you have some genuinely dramatic and exciting news to impart, you might consider holding a press conference.
- A press conference should NOT be held if there is any doubt

as to its success, or if there is no really newsworthy information to pass on.

- Choosing the right venue is important. It can be a good idea to choose an unusual setting, to make your press conference stand out from the rest.
- Try to avoid clashing with major events which are likely to tie up journalists who might otherwise attend your press conference. A good time of day is mid-morning, with the provision of coffee and light refreshments only.
- Invitations should be sent a few days in advance to named journalists. Avoid giving away so much in your invitation that the journalists don't have to come to the event itself.
- If the occasion merits it, prepare a press pack for those attending. This may include a press release, background information and photographs. Do not give these out until the end.
- TV and radio coverage can be obtained in just the same way as printed media, by sending a press release to the newsroom of the broadcaster in question.
- The best stories for TV have good news, human interest and visual appeal, and are in some way quirky or unusual.
- If you are invited to appear on television, try to find out as much as possible about the programme beforehand. Prepare in advance two or three key points which you want to get over.
- At the interview speak clearly and distinctly, avoiding any temptation to gabble. Aim to come across as sincere and enthusiastic. Above all, SMILE!
- If the interviewer rephrases your statements, make sure he gets them right, and correct them at once if not. Similarly, refute immediately any incorrect statements.
- Always remain calm and courteous, even if you feel that you are being provoked. Avoid losing your temper.
- Radio interviews are often recorded over the phone. Never give such an interview off-the-cuff. Ask the reporter if you can phone back, then take a few minutes to prepare yourself.
- When giving a radio interview, vary your pace and tone. Smile when you are speaking - listeners will hear the good humour in your voice.
- Sponsorship can be a powerful PR tool. The best known area is sports sponsorship, but other areas such as education and the arts also provide opportunities.
- You can also support local charities and other good causes. The possibilities include providing expertise and resources, donating unwanted equipment and supporting employee volunteering.
- Newsletters can be a worthwhile PR investment. They are

especially useful for service-based companies, who can use them to highlight how different clients have made use of their services.

- Accept any invitation you receive to speak in public. Find out as much as possible about your audience and their expectations, and prepare your speech carefully beforehand.
- If it is appropriate to your business, consider producing a how-to-do-it guide which customers and prospects may keep for future reference.

GLOSSARY
OF TERMS

ABOVE-THE-LINE ADVERTISING
Term used to describe press, radio, TV, cinema and outdoor advertising, which traditionally paid commission to advertising agencies on media purchases (c.f. Below-the-line).

ADVERTISING
Paid-for communications which aim to bring a business and its products or services to the attention of potential consumers, and persuade them - or start to persuade them - to buy.

ADVERTISING AGENCY
An agency which handles advertising on behalf of other businesses. The service usually includes strategic planning, copywriting and design, preparing artwork, booking advertising space, and so on.

ADVERTISING CARDS
Cards used to advertise in newsagents' windows, or, in smaller versions, for distribution in public places or door-to-door. Can be very cost-effective for some kinds of business.

ADVERTISING FEATURE
A special feature appearing in a newspaper or magazine and designed primarily to attract advertising. Typical subjects for advertising features include Christmas, Easter, Holidays, Gardens, Weddings.

ADVERTORIAL
Paid-for advertising which, at first sight, looks like editorial (q.v.). Advertorials usually have a high proportion of text, but may include one or two photos or illustrations as well.

AIDA
An acronym, short for 'Attention, Interest, Desire, Action'. AIDA sums up what every advertisement should be seeking to accomplish.

BANDED OFFER
A form of sales promotion in which two different but related products (e.g. a can of paint and a paint-brush) are sold together at a discount price.

BELOW-THE-LINE ADVERTISING
A term used to describe all types of advertising not covered by the term 'Above-the-line' (q.v.). Includes direct mail, point-of-sale advertising, leaflets and brochures, advertising cards, etc.

BENEFITS

The advantages to a consumer of buying a particular product (or service). Very important to consumers when deciding which of a range of competing products to purchase. Advertisements should highlight a product's benefits, not its features.

BODY TEXT

The main text of an advertisement, usually following a heading. The purpose of the body text is to gain the reader's interest and arouse his desire to buy.

BOGOF

Acronym for 'Buy One, Get One Free', a form of sales promotion.

BRAD

Acronym for British Rate And Data, the so-called Advertisers' Bible.

BROCHURE

A short publication including more details of a product or service than there is space for in an advertisement. Many are attractively produced, including illustrations. Brochures are typically sent or given to serious enquirers only; they are normally too expensive to use in mail shots.

CAMERA-READY ARTWORK

Master copy of an advertisement, leaflet, etc. ready to be used for printing, a.k.a. camera-ready copy (crc).

CIRCULATION

The number of copies of a publication printed or distributed.

CLASSIFIED ADVERTISEMENTS

The cheapest and simplest form of advertising. Classified ads normally consist of a few lines of text under a particular heading.

COMPETITION

A form of sales promotion intended to generate extra interest in a product and boost sales. To be legal (and not a lottery) a competition must contain an element of skill.

CONTAINER PREMIUM

A term describing the way that selling goods in a useful or attractive-looking container can help boost sales (e.g. selling beer shampoo in a beer glass).

COPY

Text provided for typesetting. The words - as opposed to photos, drawings, etc. - in an advertisement.

CORPORATE IMAGE

The image which a company presents to the outside world. A

strong, positive corporate image can be a powerful marketing tool, and large companies go to great lengths to develop and safeguard their corporate images.

COST PER THOUSAND
The cost of reaching 1,000 readers by advertising in any particular publication. Provides a crude, but nonetheless useful, means of comparing advertising costs between different media.

CUSTOMER LOYALTY SCHEME
A form of sales promotion set up by a retailer to try to retain existing customers and win new ones. Schemes operated by the main supermarket chains using 'smart cards' are a good example: customers are allotted points for every purchase they make, and can exchange these for cash, discounts or free gifts.

DIRECT MAIL
Method of advertising in which individual customers are contacted directly using mail shots.

DIRECTORIES
Publications listing suppliers of goods and services in various categories. Yellow Pages is a well-known directory in which many businesses providing a service direct to the public advertise.

DIRECT RESPONSE
A marketing method in which the manufacturer makes his offer direct to the consumer (e.g. by letter, telephone or E-mail), by-passing the traditional channels of distribution.

DISPENSERS
Hanging cards from which small items such as combs, pens and key-rings can be pulled off.

DISPLAY ADVERTISEMENTS
Advertisements, usually larger than classified, which incorporate design elements plus text. A typical display advertisement includes a heading, body text, illustration and order form.

DISPLAY OUTERS
Boxes of small items such as bars of chocolate which, when opened up, can be used to display the goods inside.

DUMP BINS
Tubs used in shops to present a quantity of a particular product.

DUMMY PACKS
Empty packs, perhaps larger than normal size, for use in POS displays.

EDITORIAL
Text written by journalists and supposedly objective, as opposed to paid-for advertising.

ENDORSEMENTS
Quotes from satisfied users, reviews, celebrities, etc. which show a product or service in a positive light. Endorsements are often used in direct mail and display advertising, where they can be highly effective (people are more inclined to believe praise coming from an 'objective' outside source).

FEATURES
Characteristics which are built into a product or service by the supplier, in the hope that potential customers will find them useful and attractive (c.f. Benefits).

FLYER
A single page advertising leaflet.

FREE GIFTS
Form of sales promotion often used in shops as a way of encouraging impulse buying, and in direct mail as a means of producing an immediate response. Free gifts are also used as a form of sales incentive for regular customers.

HANDBILL
Small advertising leaflet generally given out to people in the street or pushed through letterboxes.

HEADING
A phrase or short sentence (usually) appearing at the top of a display advertisement. Its main purpose is to attract readers' attention, particularly those readers who may have a genuine interest in purchasing your product.

'HELP-IF-NEEDED'
An advertising deal in which the publication agrees to rerun your advertisement free of charge if you do not meet your expenses from your first advertisement.

HIGHWAY SIGNS
Signs used on the side of road, usually to attract passing trade and tourists. Most highway signs require planning permission.

INSERT
A separate, pre-printed advertising leaflet or flyer inserted in a magazine or newspaper and distributed with it. Inserts can provide a highly cost-effective way of advertising some products and services.

INTERNET
A world-wide network of interconnected computers. Increasingly being used by businesses for advertising, marketing and PR, usually via the World Wide Web (q.v.).

KEYING
Means of monitoring where respondents have seen an advertisement. A simple keying device would be to include a 'department' reference in the address (e.g. an advertisement in the Weekly News might include 'Department WN' in the address).

LEAFLET
One or two-page advertising material used for mail shots, point-of-sale displays, exhibitions, door-to-door distribution, etc.

LIST BROKER
Someone who sells and/or rents mailing lists to other businesses.

LOGOTYPE
Often abbreviated to logo, this is a symbol or trademark used to represent a company. For maximum effect, logos need to be repeated in advertising, stationery, company vehicles, and so on.

MAIL-IN
An offer of a free gift if the consumer sends in proof of purchase. Cost of postage may be requested.

MAILING LIST
A list of names and addresses to be used in direct mail campaigns. Mailing lists may consist of past and present customers; they may be compiled from published sources such as directories; or they may be bought or rented from list brokers (q.v.).

MAIL SHOT
Advertising material sent by post to a potential customer. A typical mail shot includes a sales letter, brochure, order form and reply-paid envelope.

MARKETING
'The management process responsible for identifying, anticipating and satisfying customer requirements profitably' - The Institute of Marketing.

MEDIA SCHEDULE
A calendar or diary showing when publications carrying your advertisements are coming out, and the latest date advertising copy/artwork has to be with them.

MOBILES
Display devices which are suspended from the ceiling in larger shops and supermarkets. Most are made from cardboard.

MULTI-PACK
A form of sales promotion in which two or more packs of a product are sold together at a discount price. The aim is to increase the amount purchased and establish the buying habit for the product concerned.

ORDER FORM
A form in a display advertisement or mail shot for the reader to fill in his name and address and return with his order. Including an order form in advertisements has been shown to increase response rates significantly.

PENETRATION
The extent to which a publication reaches a specified target readership. For example, a magazine aimed at chartered accountants may claim an 80% penetration of its target market, i.e. 80% of all chartered accountants read it.

PERSON SPECIFICATION
A document detailing the qualities required in a job applicant, usually divided into those qualities which are essential and those which are merely desirable. Drawing up a person specification is an important preliminary to writing a job advertisement.

'PI' ('Per Inquiry')
An advertising deal in which you agree to pay the publication a fixed fee for each inquiry your advertisement brings in, in exchange for which the advertisement is printed free of charge.

POINT-OF-SALE ADVERTISING
Literally, advertising at the point of sale (typically a shop).

POSITIONING
Where a product is positioned in the market-place - the target market segment at which it is aimed. Positioning may be manipulated by many factors, including advertising, price, packaging, image, and so on.

PROOF
Single sheet of a print job, produced before the main run so that you can check for mistakes and make any necessary corrections. Complex jobs may require more than one proof stage.

PUBLICS
Term used in PR to describe the various target audiences which a business's communications must address. As well as potential customers, these may include suppliers, local residents, staff and potential staff, existing customers, and so on.

READER'S REPLY SERVICE
A pre-paid card normally included near the back of a magazine. The

card is marked with a reference number for each advertiser, and is designed to be easily detached. Readers tick or circle the reference numbers of advertisers they are interested in, and put the card in the post. When the magazine receives a completed card it forwards copies to those businesses whose reference numbers have been marked, so that they can send the readers concerned more information.

REAM
Five hundred sheets of paper.

RESPONSE RATE
In direct mail advertising, the response rate is the proportion of people responding to your offer. It is normally expressed as a percentage.

ROP. Run Of Paper
This means that your advertisement will appear in a publication anywhere they can fit it in. This is the cheapest form of display advertising, but can be rather a gamble.

SALES PROMOTION
Activity organised by a manufacturer or retailer to promote sales in the short term by giving purchasers of the product added value. Sales promotions can include price cuts, competitions, free gifts, etc.

SEEDING
The practice of including, in rented mailing lists, a number of people known personally by the hirer, so that he can check that the list is not used more than once without permission.

SEMI-DISPLAY
A form of classified advertising (q.v.) in which the advertisement is given extra emphasis by means of a border round it and possibly other design elements such as a logo or illustration.

STAND-BY ADVERTISING
An advertising deal in which advertising space which would otherwise remain unsold is made available to an advertiser at rates well below normal.

TEST MAILING
In direct mail, a test mailing is a preliminary, small-scale mail shot conducted to assess the probable level of response to the material enclosed.

USP
Unique Selling Proposition (or Point). A feature which is unique to a particular business, e.g. 'the only genuine Belgian restaurant in Rangoon'.

WORLD WIDE WEB

The part of the Internet (q.v.) usually used by businesses for advertising, marketing and PR. The World Wide Web is the most technologically sophisticated part of the Internet.

FURTHER READING

Advertising by Frank Jefkins
(Pitman Publishing, 1985)

Advertising Manager's Handbook by Robert Bly
(Jossey-Bass, Inc., 1998)

A Handbook of Advertising Techniques by Tony Harrison
(Kogan Page, 2nd edition, 1989)

Be Your Own PR Man by Michael Bland
(Kogan Page, 2nd edition, 1987)

The Blueprint Dictionary of Printing and Publishing by John
Peacock and Michael Barnard
(Blueprint Publishing Ltd, 1990)

Can You Put It On A T-Shirt? by Godfrey Howard
(David & Charles, 1991)

Cassell Guide to Written English by James Aitchison
(Cassell, 1994)

Commonsense Direct Marketing by Drayton Bird
(Kogan Page, 2nd edition, 1989)

The Complete Guide to Advertising by Torin Douglas
(QED Publishing Ltd, 1985)

Do-it-yourself Advertising by Roy Brewer
(Kogan Page, 1991)

Do Your Own Advertising by Alastair Crompton
(Business Books Ltd, 2nd edition, 1991)

Effective Advertising by H.C. Carter
(Kogan Page, 1986)

How to Be a Better Communicator by Sandy McMillan
(Kogan Page, 1996)

How to Develop and Profit From Your Creative Powers by
Michael LeBoeuf
(Piatkus, 1990)

How to Do Your Own Advertising by Michael Bennie
(How To Books Ltd, 1995)

How to Get Your Message Across by Dr David Lewis (Souvenir Press Limited, 1996)

How to Make Exhibitions Work for Your Business
by John Talbot
(Kogan Page, 1989)

How to Master Business English by Michael Bennie
(How To Books Ltd, 2nd edition, 1994)

How to Plan Direct Mail by Iain Maitland
(Cassell, 1997)

How to Plan Exhibitions by Iain Maitland
(Cassell, 1997)

How to Plan Press Advertising by Iain Maitland
(Cassell, 1997)

How to Plan Radio Advertising by Iain Maitland
(Cassell, 1997)

How to Write Articles for Profit and PR by Mel Lewis
(Kogan Page, 1989)

How to Write Business Letters by Ann Dobson
(How To Books Ltd, 1995)

Introduction to Marketing, Advertising and Public Relations
by Frank Jefkins
(Macmillan, 2nd edition, 1985)

Making Money With Classified Ads by Melvin Powers
(Wilshire Publications, USA, 1995)

Modern Marketing by Frank Jefkins
(Pitman Publishing, 1983)

Professional Communications - for a change by Hans Johnsson
(Prentice Hall, 1990)

Readymade Business Letters by Jim Dening
(Kogan Page, 1988)

Readymade Job Advertisements by Neil Wenborn
(Kogan Page, 1991)

Public Relations Made Simple by Frank Jefkins

(William Heinemann Ltd, 1982)

Sales Promotion by Julian Cummins
(Kogan Page, 1989)

Setting Up Your Own Business by Alan Pitman
(Hamlyn, 1990)

The Small Business Programme Handbook - Information to help
the growing business
(Paul Chapman Publishing Ltd, 1990)

Starting Up by Gary Jones
(Financial Times Management Books, 1998)

Successful Marketing for the Small Business by Dave Patten
(Kogan Page, 1998)

Writing To Win by Mel Lewis
(McGraw-Hill, 1987)

Writing Words That Sell by Suzan St Maur and John Butman
(Lennard Publishing, 1989)

COMPUTER-BASED TRAINING
Business Acumen: Marketing by Nick Daws
(Way Ahead Electronic Publishing, 5 Woodlands, Tebworth,
Bedfordshire, LU7 9QR, 1995)

DIY PR for Business
(CCA Software, Rayner House, 23 Higher Hillgate, Stockport,
Cheshire, SK1 3ER, 1995)

Effective Letters
(CCA Software, Rayner House, 23 Higher Hillgate, Stockport,
Cheshire, SK1 3ER, 1993)

INDEX